D1487071

LET FREEDOM REIGN

THE WORDS
OF NELSON MANDELA

LET FREEDOM REIGN
THE WORDS
OF NELSON MANDELA

Henry Russell

Foreword by André Brink

Interlink Books

An imprint of Interlink Publishing Group, Inc.
Northampton, Massachusetts

For Sara, Meredith, Fabia and Esther.

First American edition published in 2010 by
INTERLINK BOOKS
An imprint of Interlink Publishing Group, Inc.
46 Crosby Street, Northampton, Massachusetts 01060
www.interlinkbooks.com

Library of Congress Cataloging-in-Publication Data available

ISBN 978-1-56656-800-5

Printed and bound in India

10 9 8 7 6 5 4 3 2 1

To request our complete 48-page full-color catalog, please call us toll
free at 1-800-238-LINK, visit our website at www.interlinkbooks.com,
or send us an e-mail: info@interlinkbooks.com

The paper used to produce this book is sourced from sustainable forests.

Contents

Foreword by André Brink
Nelson Mandela: Myth • Man • Magician   6

Introduction   10

1. Political Awakening (1948–61)   14

2. In Captivity (1962–89)   30

3. Release and Triumph (1990–94)   74

4. President of South Africa
   (1994–99)   98

5. In Retirement (1999–)   120

Acknowledgements   136

Nelson Mandela
Myth · Man · Magician

Years ago, among the green mountains of the Languedoc region in France, on my way to Carcassonne, I turned off the main route to follow a thin little side-road which brought me to a tiny village with only one paved street. The others were mere paths that branched off randomly, left and right, some of them no more than flights of steps hewn from the solid rock. Here and there villagers were going about their immemorial business: a cobbler in his workshop, a spinning woman, a baker stacking fragrant baguettes on a shelf, a sprinkling of children playing on what passed for a village square. The little place seemed lost in time and space. It might have been a hundred years ago, an unimaginable distance from the nearest town.

In one of the tortuous little side streets, along a steep incline, I noticed in a small square window on my right, set in a stone wall that might have dated from the Middle Ages, the bright colours of a sticker not much bigger than a postcard. It said, as I approached to take a closer look: LIBÉREZ MANDELA.

It seemed so out of place, so utterly pointless. And yet, as I felt my throat contract, this was wholly necessary and inevitable and necessary: for there was, literally, no corner or nook in the wide world where Mandela was not relevant and present. Only a few years later he was indeed set free, and what an unforgettable moment that was, when he strode from Pollsmoor Prison outside the town of Paarl, hand in hand with his then wife Winnie, towards the frenzied crowds massed along the road through the vineyards, towards Cape Town, towards the waiting world. A world that could never be quite the same.

A moment of exultation. But also a moment fraught with dire possibilities. For when in 1964 Mandela had gone from the Rivonia trial to the prison on Robben Island — truly a place where a man had to abandon all hope of ever returning to the outside world — the legacy he had left behind was encapsulated in one of the truly unforgettable speeches of our modern era culminating in those ringing words: It is an ideal which I hope to live for and to achieve. But if it needs be, it is an ideal for which I am prepared to die. *During the 27 years of his captivity these words had continued to reverberate around the world: on the campuses of the USA and Western Europe, behind the Iron Curtain, in small clandestine gatherings and large auditoriums; they had acquired breadth and depth and the quality of prophecy and vision: such stuff as dreams and myth are made on. Now, emerging from prison, there was a real danger that the man could no longer match the myth. How could* anyone *live up to the expectations the world had dreamt about him: the hopes of the oppressed, the groans of the suffering, the imaginings of politicians, of the poor and the deprived all around the world, the unexpressed and inexpressible yearnings of the millions of women and men who believe that life could and should be different and more meaningful than the existence they had been relegated to?*

Mandela himself tried to make it clear that he was merely human: I stand here before you, *he said in Cape Town on 11 February 1990, in his very first speech after his release from prison,* not as a prophet but as a humble servant of you, the people. *But that was easier said than done. The miracle was that this was exactly what he achieved. He never betrayed the myth: in almost every imaginable respect he lived to the expectations of the world. But he never sacrificed his humanity – warts and all he showed humanity what a human being could do, and be. The story was told about his final journey through Europe, at the end of the first term of his presidency, when he voluntarily laid down the burden of office and went to take his leave from all the heads of state who had offered him and his people their support during his term of office; and how at the end of every exhausting day, he would summon all his secretaries (four of them, I was told, as he had too much energy for one or two), and invited them to sit on his bed before he went to sleep. 'Now tell me,' he would ask of them, 'what have I done wrong today?'*

Can anybody, by any stretch of his or her moral or mental resources, imagine any other leader acting in this manner? To Mandela it came naturally; it was not an act (even though he could be a consummate actor when occasion demanded). Because, when all was said and done, he was a man among women and men and most particularly children.

It is because of the very humanness of his humanity – for better or for worse – that the way in which Mandela assumed the burden of being a man among people transformed the very ordinariness of his being into something magical. The famed Madiba Magic *has endowed him with the almost uncanny ability to transcend the ordinary. At the time of our first free elections, Mandela made me believe:* We have achieved the extraordinary. Now we can tackle the ordinary. Because in this country we have a human being in charge. No more. And certainly no less.

Part of his humanity resided in his resolve never to accept that the struggle to which he had dedicated his life, his long walk to freedom, could ever be over. Much of his energy went into the realization of his dream for a commission in charge of truth and reconciliation. Long after many of his colleagues – including the unreliable and often unpredictable F.W. de Klerk, Mandela's second deputy president with whom Madiba had to share his Nobel Prize and to whom he had addressed some of his harshest (but eminently well-deserved) words at the end of the first day of the CODESA negotiations – had faltered in their support of this remarkable enterprise (flawed as it may have been), Mandela remained as steadfast as Table Mountain.

However reasonable and understanding and forgiving he could be in his dealings with others, there were some things he ferociously condemned whenever and wherever he encountered them: deviousness, a self-serving mentality, narrow-minded politics, a tendency not to see the wood for the trees. Mandela's burning honesty, the clarity and depth of his vision, could tolerate no mendacity or egotistic and nepotistic pettiness. In the end, when his successor, Thabo Mbeki, shamefully turned away from the war against AIDS and condoned Mugabe's excesses in Zimbabwe, Mandela did not hesitate to lambaste the man who had been his understudy. And yet there has always been in him a profound awareness of human fallibility. As a statesman he never expected perfection of others (even if he mostly demanded it of himself); he could always reason, and offer help, and forgiveness. What guided his brand of humanity has been the conviction that, In a cynical world we have become an inspiration to many. We signal that good can be achieved amongst human beings who are prepared to trust, prepared to believe in the goodness of people, *as he said in his review of the country's first 'Democratic Decade' in 2004.*

I often feel, in a time when so much of Mandela's legacy is placed in jeopardy by misguided or small-minded followers who all too often taint and distort his great vision with personal agendas and private ambitions, that if some good is ultimately to come from the South African experience, it would be because, when everything *is put to the test and* everything *is at stake, an abiding sense of loyalty to the myth, the man and the magician may yet prevail against all the odds.*

– André Brink

Introduction

Nelson Mandela, the first democratically elected black president of South Africa is celebrated for his heroic life and for his oratory. The son of Chief Henry Mandela, a minor member of the Thembu royal line, Rolihlahla Mandela was born on 18 July 1918 in Mvezo, a village in the district of Umtata, Transkei. After Mandela's father was deposed as Mvezo Chief, the family took refuge in Qunu, just south of Umtata. He was the first member of his family to receive a Western-style education. In the schools of the time, African pupils were customarily given an English name on their first day. Mandela got 'Nelson' and, although he never knew why his teacher called him that – it was possibly after Admiral Horatio Lord Nelson (1758–1805), the hero of the Battle of Trafalgar (21 October 1805) – henceforth, he always retained it in front of his original forename, which means 'he who pulls up the branch of a tree' – figuratively, 'troublemaker'.

Henry Mandela died of tuberculosis in 1927. While waiting to attain his majority at the age of 16, Nelson attended meetings held by Chief Jongintaba Dalindyebo, the acting regent, at Mqhekezweni, the provisional capital of Thembuland. There, he learned some of his earliest lessons in oratory and in achieving consensus through discussion. He later recalled the meetings as 'democracy in its purest form', where all comers were at liberty to talk without interruption about whatever was on their minds. Mandela also learned a technique for which he would become renowned: that of listening to what everyone had to say before venturing his own opinion or making a judgement. He later recalled the Chief's axiom that a leader is like a shepherd who always stays behind the flock, letting the most nimble go on ahead; the other sheep follow without realizing that they are being directed from behind.

Mandela attended the University College of Fort Hare at Alice in the Eastern Cape Province and there heard an address by Jan Smuts (1870–1950; prime minister of South Africa 1919–24 and 1939–48). Mandela was impressed by the old statesman's authoritative presence and gained strength from his evident difficulties in speaking English (Smuts's first language was Afrikaans; Mandela's was Xhosa).

Mandela then took a law degree at the University of Witwatersrand in Johannesburg, graduating in 1939. Four years later, he joined the African

National Congress (ANC), and in 1944 became a founder member of its Youth League. His politics were further radicalized in 1948, when the Afrikaner-dominated National Party won the whites-only general election and instituted apartheid, a strictly codified policy of racial segregation which gave the minority white population far greater rights and privileges than the black majority.

Having renounced his claim to the chieftainship of the Tembu, Mandela opened a law firm with his lifelong friend and fellow ANC member Oliver Tambo (1917–93) in 1952. In that same year, Mandela took a leading role in the ANC's Defiance Campaign, in which thousands of South Africans peacefully refused to obey apartheid laws. The campaign, which carried on into 1953, led to the imprisonment of more than 8,000 protesters. In 1955, Mandela was one of the authors of the Freedom Charter, which called for equal rights for all South Africans. In 1956, he was arrested and charged with trying to overthrow the South African state by violent means. The ensuing treason trial, which lasted until 1961, ended in the acquittal of all the accused.

During the protracted court proceedings, throughout which the defendants were bailed, Mandela divorced Evelyn Ntoko Mase (1922–2004), his wife since 1944, and married Nomzamo Winifred (Winnie) Madikizela (b. 1936); they were to divorce in 1996.

In 1960, the Sharpeville massacre, in which 69 unarmed black demonstrators were killed by South African police, and the subsequent outlawing of the ANC, convinced Mandela that a fair and free society could not be achieved by peaceful protest alone. Shortly after the trial, Mandela became leader of Umkhonto we Sizwe ('Spear of the Nation', see page 31), the new military wing of the ANC, which was formed to carry out acts of sabotage against the state.

After 17 months in hiding, Mandela was captured in 1962 and sentenced to 5 years' imprisonment. While he was in jail, the authorities found new evidence to link him and others to Umkhonto we Sizwe. The subsequent legal proceedings became known as the Rivonia Trial, after the suburb of Johannesburg in which police had raided a safe house. They ended in 1964 with Mandela's conviction on all charges. At the age of 46, he was sentenced to life imprisonment without parole. Mandela spent the next 18 years in Robben Island Prison, off Cape Town. In 1982, he was transferred to the maximum security Pollsmoor Prison, where he remained until 1988, when he was taken to hospital for what turned out to be tuberculosis (TB). In December 1988, Mandela was moved to Victor Verster Prison in Paarl.

Throughout his imprisonment, Mandela retained wide support among South Africa's black population, and his case became a worldwide cause célèbre. As the apartheid regime was gradually weakened by international pressure, the government of F.W. de Klerk softened its attitude towards segregation. On 11 February 1990 Mandela was released after 27 years behind bars. On 2 March he was appointed deputy president of the ANC, becoming its president in July 1991. Mandela and de Klerk worked to end apartheid and bring about a peaceful transition to non-racial democracy in South Africa. In 1993 they were jointly awarded the Nobel Peace Prize.

In April 1994 South Africa held its first free, one-adult one-vote election, which was won by Mandela and the ANC. As president, Mandela introduced a new democratic constitution together with numerous measures to improve the lives of the country's black population. The greatest landmark of his term of office is generally agreed to have been the establishment of the Truth and Reconciliation Commission (1995–98), which investigated human rights violations under apartheid. When his term of office ended in 1999, Mandela, aged 81, retired from active politics.

There is no doubt that his deeds alone should guarantee Nelson Mandela a place in the pantheon of great political figures. But his stature is further increased by his writings, especially the autobiography Long Walk to Freedom (1994), and above all by his speeches, some of which are featured in this book.

The basis of great oratory is neither fluency nor stridency – these are the attributes of the demagogue. The true foundation, as Cicero (106–43 BC) noted in De oratore, is knowledge, and all Mandela's speeches – from the greatest landmarks to the most informal scripted remarks – reveal in-depth research, together with a lawyer's mastery of his brief.

Most public speakers, like artists, are part of a tradition. Some imitate the style of those who have influenced them; others invoke the names of their masters or make unmistakable allusions to them. In addition to Chief Jongintaba Dalindyebothe and Smuts, Mandela was impressed by the broadcasts of Winston Churchill (1874–1965; British prime minister 1940–5 and 1951–5). He was also influenced by the life and speeches of Mohandas

'Mahatma' Karamchand Gandhi (1869–1948), the leader of the Indian nationalist movement against British rule and the model for all who seek to achieve political and social progress through non-violent protest and passive resistance.

Then, from 1962 to 1990, almost the only political voice that Mandela heard – apart from odd conversations with prisoners and warders – was his own. Mandela's largely self-taught oratory style is perhaps the finest illustration of the dictum of Georges-Louis Leclerc de Buffon (1707–88): 'Le style est l'homme même' – Style is the man himself.

– Henry Russell,
London, 2009

Chapter 1

Political Awakening (1948–61)

In 1948, the National Party won the Europeans-only general election and immediately introduced a massive legislative programme that consolidated white supremacy through apartheid (Afrikaans: 'apartness'). Racial segregation was already well-established in South Africa, but the National Party now codified and enshrined it with draconian laws. The Population Registration Act of 1950 classified all South Africans as Bantu (all black Africans), Coloured (those of mixed race), or White. A fourth category – Asian (Indian and Pakistani) – was later added.

The Group Areas Act in the same year established residential and business sections in urban areas for each race, and members of other races were barred from living, operating businesses, or owning land in them. Thus, 80 percent of the land was given over to the whites, who comprised only 20 percent of the population. Mixed marriages were forbidden, along with any sexual relations between the races. Public facilities were segregated and non-whites were denied direct governmental representation.

Meanwhile, Mandela grew in stature as a political leader. Public speaking did not come easily to him, and the temperate nature of his mature oratory was only gradually achieved. As he later admitted, '*I was something of a rabble-rousing speaker. I liked to incite an audience*'. One day, at a rally in Freedom Square, Johannesburg, he overstepped the mark, saying that the time for passive resistance had ended, that non-violence was a useless strategy and could never overturn a white minority regime bent on retaining its power at any cost. He added: '*At the end of the day... violence was the only weapon that would destroy apartheid and we must be prepared, in the near future, to use that weapon...*'.

He may have been right, but he had spoken too soon. He was reprimanded by the National Executive of the ANC. From that moment until his acquittal at the end of the treason trial, Mandela moderated his language as his politics became more extreme. His rhetoric becomes circumlocutory. The questions '*How are we going to react?*' (p. 24) and '*Can the oppressed people count on the Liberal Party as an ally?*' (p. 29) remain unanswered but those who could read the political runes saw that Mandela was referring to a very particular kind of action that most people dared not name.

Lisping in Numbers

Presidential Address at the Annual Conference
of the ANC Youth League,
Bloemfontein, December 1951

That Mandela had learned an important early lesson may be seen in the following extracts from his long speech to the ANC Youth League just before the start of the Defiance Campaign Against Unjust Laws – the largest non-violent resistance initiative ever seen in South Africa and the first to be pursued jointly by all racial groups under the leadership of the ANC and the South African Indian Congress (SAIC). The script shows the early coalescence of his oratorical style: mastery of detail; avoidance of inflammatory language, in spite of his apocalyptic vision of the consequences of apartheid for South African society; clear, logical exposition of policy, and, at the end of the opening paragraph, an admixture of humour. His speech also, in spite of the odd omitted preposition, conjunction and article, shows a growing mastery of English – his second language.

It is always a most difficult task to deliver a presidential address to an organization such as ours. One is expected to give as comprehensive a picture as possible of the political situation, both nationally and internationally. Then included must be the review of the organizational strength and power of the movement and the progress it has made in its efforts to carry the people to victory. Lastly, some indication must be given to the reply the organization must make to the situation having regard to the preceding analyses. Quite clearly it is not possible to do justice to all these, and yet a presidential address in which anyone of them is missing is not worthy of the name. I have [heard] it said that Dr. [Kwame] Nkrumah [founding president of Ghana, 1957–66] addresses conferences for five hours. I do not intend to break his record.

Mankind as a whole is today standing on the threshold of great events – events that at times seem to threaten its very existence...

In Africa the colonial powers... are attempting with the help of the notorious American ruling class to maintain colonial rule and oppression. Millions of pounds are pouring into the continent in the form of capital for the exploitation of our resources in the sole interests of the imperialist powers. So-called geological and archaeological expeditions are roaming the continent ostensibly engaged in gathering material for the advancement of science and the furtherance of humanity but being in reality the advance guard of American penetration. It is important for us and for the African people as a whole to realize that but for the support of American finance it would have been difficult if not impossible for the Western colonial powers to maintain rule in Africa, nor indeed anywhere in the world. In thinking of the direct enemies of the African people, namely, Great Britain, Spain, France, Portugal, Italy and S.A. [South Africa], we must never forget the indirect enemy, the infinitely more dangerous enemy who sustains all those with loans, capital, and arms.

In common with people all over the world,
humanity in Africa is fighting these forces...
These are hopeful signs, but precisely because
the African liberation movement is gaining
strength the rulers will become more brutal and,
in their desperation, will practice all manner of
deception in order to stay on at any rate to
postpone the day of final victory. But history
is on the side of the oppressed.

Here in South Africa the situation is an extremely
grave and serious one... The situation is developing
[in] the direction of an openly fascist state... The
acts passed by the government ... provide the
ready-made framework for the establishment of the
fascist state...

But the development of fascism in the country is
an indication of the fear they have [of] the people.
They realize that their world is a dying world and
that the appearance of impregnable strength is a
mere façade. The new world is the one in which
the oppressed Africans live. They see before their
eyes the growth of a mighty people's movement.
The struggles of 1950 were an indication that
the leaders of the Africans and their allies were
fully aware of the weakest link in the chain of
white supremacy. The labour power of the African
people is a force which when fully tapped is
going to sweep the people to power in the land
of their birth. True, the struggle will be a bitter
one. Leaders will be deported, imprisoned, and
even shot. The government will terrorize the
people and their leaders in an effort to halt the
forward march; ordinary forms of organization

will be rendered impossible. But the spirit of the people cannot be crushed, and no matter what happens to the present leadership, new leaders will arise like mushrooms till full victory is won...

Sons and daughters of Africa, I do not think we differ concerning our ideas of the aims of African nationalism in Africa. In any case the very nature of [the] national movement to which we belong makes it impossible to expect [an] absolutely identical approach...

Then we have to design on concrete steps to be taken to deal with the situation that has arisen as a result of the Suppression of Communism Amendment Act. How are we going to react to the liquidation of Congress leaders as [a] result of this act? And how are the operations going to be carried on in the event of our being banned?...

We have to discuss measures [for] the creation of strong nuclei of active workers in the struggle on the proper organization of the League and the Congress [and] the elimination of unredeemable reactionaries, which work has proceeded quite far in certain areas. We have to consider measures to eliminate the looseness and lack of discipline in the movement and also the cultivation of a serious approach to the struggle. In this context we have to examine various tactics and weapons in our struggle, including boycott, civil disobedience, and strikes.

Sons and daughters of Africa, our tasks are mighty indeed, but I have abundant faith in our ability to reply to the challenge posed by the situation. Under the slogan of FULL DEMOCRATIC RIGHTS IN SOUTH AFRICA NOW, we must march forward into victory.

Spreading the Word
Liberation *magazine, June 1953*

Although never a communist, Mandela was twice 'banned' under the 1950 Suppression of Communism Act, an apartheid law that enabled the police to prevent dissidents from meeting more than one person at a time and visiting various public places and educational institutions. Nothing the banned person said or wrote could be quoted in the press or used for publication. There was no appeal against a banning order. One of Mandela's bans prevented him from attending the annual convention of the ANC (Transvaal). His speech had to be delivered by a delegate.

In between arrests and bans, Mandela addressed numerous rallies and wrote a number of articles. The following extract is from 'Searchlight on the Liberal Party', which was published in the monthly periodical *Liberation* in response to those who feared that the ANC was becoming a communist catspaw. Although the trenchant legalese of the piece drove a wedge between the two anti-apartheid groups, it was an important restatement of Mandela's clarity of vision and firmness of purpose. And to keen political observers, the use in the final sentence of the word *'struggle'* suggested that the velvet glove might now contain a fist.

The Liberal Party constitution purports to uphold the 'essential dignity of every human being irrespective of race, colour, or creed, and the maintenance of his fundamental rights'. It expresses itself in favour of the 'right of every human being to develop to the fullest extent of which he is capable consistent with the rights of others'.

The new party's statement of principles thus far contents itself with the broad generalizations without any attempt to interpret them or define their practical application in the South African context. It then proceeds to announce 'that no person (should) be debarred from participation in the government or other democratic processes of the country by reason only of race, colour, or creed'. But here the neo-Liberals abandon the safe ground of generalization and stipulate explicitly 'that political rights based on a common franchise roll be extended to all SUITABLY QUALIFIED persons. This question-begging formulation will not for long enable our Liberals to evade the fundamental issue: which persons are 'suitably qualified'?

The democratic principle is 'one adult, one vote'. The Liberals obviously differ from this well-known conception. They are, therefore, obliged to state an alternative theory of their own. This they have, so far, failed to do. The African National Congress… [stands] for votes for all… Does the Liberal Party support this demand? Historical reality demands a plain and unequivocal answer...

In South Africa, where the entire population is almost split into two hostile camps in consequence of the policy of racial discrimination, and where recent political events have made the struggle between oppressor and oppressed more acute, there can be no middle course. The fault of the Liberals – and this spells their doom – is to attempt to strike just such a course. They believe in criticizing and condemning the Government for its reactionary policies but they are afraid to identify themselves with the people and to assume the task of mobilizing that social force capable of lifting the struggle to higher levels.

The Liberals' credo states that to achieve their objects the party will employ 'only democratic and constitutional means and will oppose all forms of totalitarianism such as communism and fascism'. Talk of democratic and constitutional means can only have a basis in reality for those people who enjoy democratic and constitutional rights.

We must accept the fact that in our country we cannot win one single victory of political freedom without overcoming a desperate resistance on the part of the Government, and that victory will not come of itself but only as a result of a bitter struggle by the oppressed people for the overthrow of racial discrimination. This means that we are committed to struggle to mobilize from our ranks the forces capable of waging a determined and militant struggle against all forms of reaction. The theory that we can sit with folded arms and wait for a future parliament to legislate for the 'essential dignity of every human being irrespective of race, colour, or creed' is crass perversion of elementary principles of political struggle. No organization whose interests are identical with those of the toiling masses will advocate conciliation to win its demands.

To propose in the South African context that democrats limit themselves to constitutional means of struggle is to ask the people to submit to laws enacted by a minority parliament whose composition is essentially a denial of democracy to the overwhelming majority of the population. It means that we must obey a Constitution which debars the majority from participating in the government and other democratic processes of the country by reason only of race, colour, or creed. It implies in practice that we must carry passes and permit the violation of the essential dignity of a human being...

The real question is: in the general struggle for political rights can the oppressed people count on the Liberal Party as an ally?... Rather than attempt the costly, dubious, and dangerous task of crushing the non-European mass movement by force, they would seek to divert it with fine words and promises and to divide it by giving concessions and bribes to a privileged minority (the 'suitably qualified' voters, perhaps). It becomes clear, therefore, that the high-sounding principles enunciated by the Liberal Party, though apparently

democratic and progressive in form, are essentially
reactionary in content. They stand not for the
freedom of the people but for the adoption
of more subtle systems of oppression and
exploitation. Though they talk of liberty and
human dignity they are subordinate henchmen
of the ruling circles. They stand for the retention
of the cheap labour system and of the subordinate
colonial status of the non-European masses
together with the Nationalist Government whose
class interests are identical with theirs. In practice
they acquiesce in the slavery of the people, low
wages, mass unemployment, the squalid tenements
in the locations and shanty-towns.

We of the non-European liberation movement
are not racialists. We are convinced that there
are thousands of honest democrats among the
White population who are prepared to take up
a firm and courageous stand for unconditional
equality, for the complete renunciation of 'White
supremacy'. To them we extend the hand of
sincere friendship and brotherly alliance. But
no true alliance can be built on the shifting
sands of evasions, illusions, and opportunism.
We insist on presenting the conditions which
make it reasonable to fight for freedom. The
only sure road to this goal leads through the
uncompromising and determined mass struggle
for the overthrow of fascism and the establishment
of democratic forms of government.

The State Strikes the First Blow
5 December 1956

In 1955, the ANC, in alliance with radical whites, Coloureds, and Indians, issued a Freedom Charter for non-racial social democracy. At the end of the following year, in dawn raids throughout South Africa, police arrested nearly all the leaders of the most prominent anti-apartheid organizations. Among the 156 people detained were Mandela, ANC President Albert Luthuli (1898–1967) and Walter Sisulu (1912–2003). They were all charged with '*Hoogverraad*' (high treason). Preliminary hearings began almost immediately but were not concluded until January 1958, when charges against 61 of the accused were dropped.

The remaining 95 men and women went on trial on 3 August 1958. The case against many of them was flimsy, and charges were later dropped against another 65. The last 30 accused were all ANC members. After 31 months, the judge interrupted the defence's closing address to declare that, while he accepted the ANC was working to replace the government and had used illegal means of protest during the Defiance Campaign, the prosecution had failed to show that the ANC was using violence to overthrow the government. The accused were, therefore, not guilty of treason and all of the defendants were discharged.

During the trial, Mandela and Evelyn divorced after 13 years of marriage, during which she had borne him four children. The marriage was strained to breaking point by his frequent absences and his devotion to the ANC cause, while she had become a Jehovah's Witness, a faith that proscribes political activism. In 1958, Mandela married Nomzamo Winifred ('Winnie') Madikizela.

Despite the acquittals, Nelson Mandela did not believe that this was the end of the state's attempts to smash the ANC.

> … [T]he result only made the state more bitter towards us. The lesson they took away was not that we had legitimate grievances but that they needed to be far more ruthless.

> I did not regard the verdict as a vindication of the legal system or evidence that a black man could get a fair trial in a white man's court. It was the right verdict and a just one, but it was largely as a result of a superior defence team and the fair-mindedness of these particular judges.

The Sharpeville Massacre
21 March 1960

A crowd of 20,000 Africans gathered in the black township of Sharpeville – near Vereeniging, about 30 miles (50 km) south of Johannesburg – to protest against the pass laws, which obliged non-whites to carry documents authorizing their presence in restricted areas.

Police opened fire with submachine guns, killing 69 of the demonstrators and wounding a further 180, including 50 women and children.

The Sharpeville massacre prompted the imposition of martial law and confirmed Mandela's decision — made during the treason trial — that, when he walked free from the court, he would not return to his home but go underground. It also made him certain that the time for peaceful protest was at an end, as is evident in the words that follow.

> ... I did not mask the fact that I believed a new day was dawning. I said [to ANC colleagues], '*If the government reaction is to crush by naked force our non-violent struggle, we will have to reconsider our tactics. In my mind we are closing a chapter on this question of a non-violent policy*'. It was a grave declaration, and I knew it. I was criticized by [the ANC] Executive for making that remark before it was discussed by the organization, but sometimes one must go public with an idea to push a reluctant organization in the direction you want it to go.

Chapter 2
In Captivity
(1962–89)

After his acquittal in the treason trial, Nelson Mandela became leader of *Umkhonto we Sizwe* (abbreviated to MK; English translation, *Spear of the Nation*). The decision to establish this military wing of the ANC was not taken lightly. From its foundation in 1912, the ANC had treated non-violence as a core principle, beyond question or debate. However, the Sharpeville massacre had brought despair to many black South Africans and they felt that there was now no alternative response to their oppression. Mandela shared this view, but remained adamant that, while sabotage was acceptable, there should be no attacks on people.

Nevertheless, there was, at first, no clear consensus that armed resistance was the best, or even a practical, policy to pursue. It was suggested that the ANC leaders should go into exile, and some of them did indeed leave the country, including Oliver Tambo, who left South Africa in 1960 for London, where he set up an external wing of the ANC. However, Mandela rejected this course, asserting: *'The struggle is my life. I will continue freedom fighting until the end of my days'.*

However, the need to secure financial backing and logistical support for the ANC struggle necessitated clandestine journeys abroad. Back in South Africa, Mandela disguised his appearance. He could not return to his own home – where his second wife, Winnie, was now raising their two daughters (Zenani b. 1959 and Zindzi b. 1960) alone – or to that of his mother, for fear of arrest. Instead, he stayed in a succession of safe houses, moving only under the cover of darkness – an often perilous strategy.

'I am prepared to die'
Pretoria Supreme Court, 20 April 1964

After 17 months of evading the authorities, Mandela was arrested on 5 August 1962 as he was driven by Cecil Williams, a white theatre director and fellow activist, through Cedara, a small town in KwaZulu–Natal. He was charged with *'inciting African workers to strike and leaving South Africa without valid travel documents'*. These were serious offences under the apartheid regime and carried maximum penalties of 10 years' imprisonment. Nevertheless, they came as something of a relief to Mandela, because they showed that the police were still unaware of his role in the MK.

On 25 October 1962, Mandela was sentenced to 5 years in prison. He served the first part of his

sentence in Pretoria jail before being transferred
in May 1963 to the maximum security prison on
Robben Island in the Atlantic Ocean, 6 miles (10
km) off Cape Town.

On 11 July 1963, the police raided Liliesleaf Farm
in Rivonia, a fashionable suburb of Johannesburg.
There, they found arms and military equipment at
what had been the secret headquarters of the MK
and evidence to link Mandela to the organization.

The imprisoned Mandela and 18 other men were
indicted on charges of sabotage, treason and
violent conspiracy. What became known as the
'Rivonia Trial' began on 9 October 1963. More
than six months later, at the start of the defence
case, Mandela made a four-hour statement from
the dock that is widely regarded as one of
the greatest speeches of all time. The power of
his address derives not from verbal pyrotechnics
but in part from the temperate language with
which he untangles his version of events from
that of the prosecution.

Mandela uses this opportunity to highlight the
hardships facing the African population under
the apartheid regime. He remonstrates against
poverty, lack of education, employment
discrimination and the highly inflammatory pass
laws – which required black Africans to carry
identity documents detailing their employment
history and rights of residence and were designed
to control their movement. Mandela's repetition
of the key phrase '*Africans want...*' emphasized
these issues and reaffirmed his message.

Mandela spoke in the knowledge that the maximum penalty for the crimes with which he was accused was death. The following is an extract from that speech.

I am the First Accused...

At the outset, I want to say that the suggestion made by the State in its opening that the struggle in South Africa is under the influence of foreigners or communists is wholly incorrect. I have done whatever I did, both as an individual and as a leader of my people, because of my experience in South Africa and my own proudly felt African background, and not because of what any outsider might have said...

... I must deal immediately and at some length with the question of violence. Some of the things so far told to the Court are true and some are untrue. I do not, however, deny that I planned sabotage. I did not plan it in a spirit of recklessness, nor because I have any love of violence. I planned it as a result of a calm and sober assessment of the political situation that had arisen after many years of tyranny, exploitation, and oppression of my people by the Whites.

I admit immediately that I was one of the persons who helped to form *Umkhonto we Sizwe*, and that I played a prominent role in its affairs until I was arrested in August 1962.

... I have already mentioned that I was one of the persons who helped to form *Umkhonto*. I, and the

others who started the organization, did so for
two reasons. Firstly, we believed that as a result
of Government policy, violence by the African
people had become inevitable, and that unless
responsible leadership was given to canalize
and control the feelings of our people, there
would be outbreaks of terrorism which would
produce an intensity of bitterness and hostility
between the various races of this country which
is not produced even by war. Secondly, we felt
that without violence there would be no way
open to the African people to succeed in their
struggle against the principle of white supremacy.
All lawful modes of expressing opposition to this
principle had been closed by legislation, and we
were placed in a position in which we had either
to accept a permanent state of inferiority, or to
defy the Government. We chose to defy the law.
We first broke the law in a way which avoided
any recourse to violence; when this form was
legislated against, and then the Government
resorted to a show of force to crush opposition
to its policies, only then did we decide to answer
violence with violence.

But the violence which we chose to adopt was
not terrorism. We who formed *Umkhonto* were
all members of the African National Congress,
and had behind us the ANC tradition of non-
violence and negotiation as a means of solving
political disputes. We believe that South Africa
belongs to all the people who live in it, and not
to one group, be it black or white. We did not
want an interracial war, and tried to avoid it to
the last minute…

The African National Congress [ANC] was formed
in 1912 to defend the rights of the African people
which had been seriously curtailed by the South
Africa Act, and which were then being threatened
by the Native Land Act. For 37 years – that is until
1949 – it adhered strictly to a constitutional
struggle. It put forward demands and resolutions;
it sent delegations to the Government in the
belief that African grievances could be settled
through peaceful discussion and that Africans could
advance gradually to full political rights. But White
Governments remained unmoved, and the rights
of Africans became less instead of becoming
greater. In the words of my leader, Chief Luthuli,
who became president of the ANC in 1952, and
who was later awarded the Nobel Peace Prize:

'*Who will deny that 30 years of my life have been
spent knocking in vain, patiently, moderately, and
modestly at a closed and barred door? What have
been the fruits of moderation? The past 30 years have
seen the greatest number of laws restricting our rights
and progress, until today we have reached a stage
where we have almost no rights at all*'.

Even after 1949, the ANC remained determined
to avoid violence. At this time, however, there
was a change from the strictly constitutional means
of protest which had been employed in the past.
The change was embodied in a decision which
was taken to protest against apartheid legislation
by peaceful, but unlawful, demonstrations against
certain laws. Pursuant to this policy the ANC
launched the Defiance Campaign, in which I
was placed in charge of volunteers. This campaign

was based on the principles of passive resistance.
More than 8,500 people defied apartheid laws
and went to jail. Yet there was not a single
instance of violence in the course of this campaign
on the part of any defier. I and 19 colleagues
were convicted for the role which we played in
organizing the campaign, but our sentences were
suspended mainly because the Judge found that
discipline and non-violence had been stressed
throughout. This was the time when the volunteer
section of the ANC was established, and when the
word 'Amadelakufa' [self-sacrifice for the good of
the nation] was first used: this was the time when
the volunteers were asked to take a pledge to
uphold certain principles. Evidence dealing with
volunteers and their pledges has been introduced
into this case, but completely out of context. The
volunteers were not, and are not, the soldiers of
a black army pledged to fight a civil war against
the whites. They were, and are, dedicated workers
who are prepared to lead campaigns initiated
by the ANC to distribute leaflets, to organize
strikes, or do whatever the particular campaign
required. They are called volunteers because they
volunteer to face the penalties of imprisonment
and whipping which are now prescribed by the
legislature for such acts.

During the Defiance Campaign, the Public Safety
Act and the Criminal Law Amendment Act were
passed. These Statutes provided harsher penalties
for offences committed by way of protests against
laws. Despite this, the protests continued and the
ANC adhered to its policy of non-violence. In
1956, 156 leading members of the Congress

Alliance [joint anti-apartheid movement under
the direction of the ANC], including myself,
were arrested on a charge of high treason and
charges under the Suppression of Communism
Act. The non-violent policy of the ANC was put
in issue by the State, but when the Court gave
judgement some five years later, it found that the
ANC did not have a policy of violence. We were
acquitted on all counts, which included a count
that the ANC sought to set up a communist state
in place of the existing regime. The Government
has always sought to label all its opponents as
communists. This allegation has been repeated
in the present case, but as I will show, the
ANC is not, and never has been, a communist
organization.

In 1960 there was the shooting at Sharpeville,
which resulted in the proclamation of a state
of emergency and the declaration of the ANC as
an unlawful organization. My colleagues and I,
after careful consideration, decided that we would
not obey this decree. The African people were
not part of the Government and did not make the
laws by which they were governed. We believed
in the words of the Universal Declaration of
Human Rights [1948 UN's policy document;
the foundation of international human rights' law],
that '*the will of the people shall be the basis of authority
of the Government*', and for us to accept the banning
was equivalent to accepting the silencing of the
Africans for all time. The ANC refused to dissolve,
but instead went underground. We believed it was
our duty to preserve this organization which had
been built up with almost 50 years of unremitting

toil. I have no doubt that no self-respecting
White political organization would disband
itself if declared illegal by a government in
which it had no say.

In 1960 the Government held a referendum
which led to the establishment of the Republic.
Africans, who constituted approximately 70
percent of the population of South Africa, were
not entitled to vote, and were not even consulted
about the proposed constitutional change. All
of us were apprehensive of our future under the
proposed White Republic, and a resolution was
taken to hold an All-In African Conference to
call for a National Convention, and to organize
mass demonstrations on the eve of the unwanted
Republic, if the Government failed to call the
Convention. The conference was attended by
Africans of various political persuasions. I was
the Secretary of the conference and undertook to
be responsible for organizing the national stay-at-
home which was subsequently called to coincide
with the declaration of the Republic. As all strikes
by Africans are illegal, the person organizing such
a strike must avoid arrest. I was chosen to be this
person, and consequently I had to leave my home
and family and my practice and go into hiding to
avoid arrest.

The stay-at-home, in accordance with ANC
policy, was to be a peaceful demonstration.
Careful instructions were given to organizers
and members to avoid any recourse to violence.
The Government's answer was to introduce new
and harsher laws, to mobilize its armed forces,

and to send Saracens [British military armoured personnel carriers], armed vehicles, and soldiers into the townships in a massive show of force designed to intimidate the people. This was an indication that the Government had decided to rule by force alone, and this decision was a milestone on the road to *Umkhonto*.

Some of this may appear irrelevant to this trial. In fact, I believe none of it is irrelevant because it will, I hope, enable the Court to appreciate the attitude eventually adopted by the various persons and bodies concerned in the National Liberation Movement. When I went to jail in 1962, the dominant idea was that loss of life should be avoided. I now know that this was still so in 1963.

I must return to June 1961. What were we, the leaders of our people, to do? Were we to give in to the show of force and the implied threat against future action, or were we to fight it and, if so, how?

… We of the ANC had always stood for a non-racial democracy, and we shrank from any action which might drive the races further apart than they already were. But the hard facts were that 50 years of non-violence had brought the African people nothing but more and more repressive legislation, and fewer and fewer rights. It may not be easy for this Court to understand, but it is a fact that for a long time the people had been talking of violence – of the day when they would fight the White man and win back their country –

and we, the leaders of the ANC, had nevertheless always prevailed upon them to avoid violence and to pursue peaceful methods...

It must not be forgotten that by this time violence had, in fact, become a feature of the South African political scene... Each disturbance pointed clearly to the inevitable growth among Africans of the belief that violence was the only way out – it showed that a Government which uses force to maintain its rule teaches the oppressed to use force to oppose it. Already small groups had arisen in the urban areas and were spontaneously making plans for violent forms of political struggle. There now arose a danger that these groups would adopt terrorism against Africans, as well as Whites, if not properly directed...

At the beginning of June 1961, after a long and anxious assessment of the South African situation, I, and some colleagues, came to the conclusion that as violence in this country was inevitable, it would be unrealistic and wrong for African leaders to continue preaching peace and non-violence at a time when the Government met our peaceful demands with force.

This conclusion was not easily arrived at. It was only when all else had failed, when all channels of peaceful protest had been barred to us, that the decision was made to embark on violent forms of political struggle, and to form *Umkhonto we Sizwe*. We did so not because we desired such a course, but solely because the Government had left us with no other choice. In the *Manifesto of*

Umkhonto published on 16 December 1961, which is Exhibit AD, we said:

> '*The time comes in the life of any nation when there remain only two choices – submit or fight. That time has now come to South Africa. We shall not submit and we have no choice but to hit back by all means in our power in defence of our people, our future, and our freedom*'.

This was our feeling in June of 1961 when we decided to press for a change in the policy of the National Liberation Movement. I can only say that I felt morally obliged to do what I did.

We who had taken this decision started to consult leaders of various organizations, including the ANC...

... in view of this situation I have described, the ANC was prepared to depart from its 50-year-old policy of non-violence to this extent that it would no longer disapprove of properly controlled violence. Hence members who undertook such activity would not be subject to disciplinary action by the ANC.

... As a result of this decision, *Umkhonto* was formed in November 1961. When we took this decision, and subsequently formulated our plans, the ANC heritage of non-violence and racial harmony was very much with us. We felt that the country was drifting towards a civil war in which Blacks and Whites would fight each other. We viewed the situation with alarm. Civil war

could mean the destruction of what the ANC
stood for; with civil war, racial peace would be
more difficult than ever to achieve…

Four forms of violence were possible. There
is sabotage, there is guerrilla warfare, there is
terrorism, and there is open revolution. We
chose to adopt the first method and to exhaust
it before taking any other decision.

In the light of our political background the choice
was a logical one. Sabotage did not involve loss of
life, and it offered the best hope for future race
relations. Bitterness would be kept to a minimum
and, if the policy bore fruit, democratic government
could become a reality…

… We believed that South Africa depended to a
large extent on foreign capital and foreign trade.
We felt that planned destruction of power
plants, and interference with rail and telephone
communications, would tend to scare away capital
from the country, make it more difficult for goods
from the industrial areas to reach the seaports on
schedule, and would in the long run be a heavy
drain on the economic life of the country, thus
compelling the voters of the country to reconsider
their position.

Attacks on the economic lifelines of the country
were to be linked with sabotage on Government
buildings and other symbols of apartheid. These
attacks would serve as a source of inspiration to
our people. In addition, they would provide an
outlet for those people who were urging the

adoption of violent methods and would enable
us to give concrete proof to our followers that
we had adopted a stronger line and were fighting
back against Government violence.

In addition, if mass action were successfully
organized, and mass reprisals taken, we felt
that sympathy for our cause would be roused
in other countries, and that greater pressure
would be brought to bear on the South
African Government.

This then was the plan. *Umkhonto* was to perform
sabotage, and strict instructions were given to its
members right from the start, that on no account
were they to injure or kill people in planning or
carrying out operations...

Umkhonto had its first operation on 16 December
1961, when Government buildings in Johannesburg,
Port Elizabeth and Durban were attacked. The
selection of targets is proof of the policy to which
I have referred. Had we intended to attack life
we would have selected targets where people
congregated and not empty buildings and power
stations...

The *Manifesto of Umkhonto* was issued on the day
that operations commenced. The response to our
actions and *Manifesto* among the white population
was characteristically violent. The Government
threatened to take strong action, and called upon
its supporters to stand firm and to ignore the
demands of the Africans. The Whites failed to
respond by suggesting change; they responded

to our call by suggesting the *laager* [Afrikaans: 'defensive encirclement'].

In contrast, the response of the Africans was one of encouragement. Suddenly there was hope again. Things were happening. People in the townships became eager for political news. A great deal of enthusiasm was generated by the initial successes, and people began to speculate on how soon freedom would be obtained.

But we in *Umkhonto* weighed up the white response with anxiety. The lines were being drawn. The whites and blacks were moving into separate camps, and the prospects of avoiding a civil war were made less. The white newspapers carried reports that sabotage would be punished by death. If this was so, how could we continue to keep Africans away from terrorism?

Already scores of Africans had died as a result of racial friction. In 1920 when the famous leader, Masabala, was held in Port Elizabeth jail, 24 of a group of Africans who had gathered to demand his release were killed by the police and white civilians. In 1921, more than 100 Africans died in the Bulhoek affair [incident in which police opened fire on black squatters in the Eastern Cape]. In 1924 over 200 Africans were killed when the Administrator of South-West Africa [modern Namibia] led a force against a group which had rebelled against the imposition of dog tax. On 1 May 1950, 18 Africans died as a result of police shootings during the strike. On 21 March 1960, 69 unarmed Africans died at Sharpeville.

How many more Sharpevilles would there be in
the history of our country? And how many more
Sharpevilles could the country stand without
violence and terror becoming the order of the
day? And what would happen to our people
when that stage was reached?

In the long run we felt certain we must succeed,
but at what cost to ourselves and the rest of the
country? And if this happened, how could black
and white ever live together again in peace and
harmony? These were the problems that faced us,
and these were our decisions.

Experience convinced us that rebellion would
offer the Government limitless opportunities
for the indiscriminate slaughter of our people.
But it was precisely because the soil of South
Africa is already drenched with the blood of
innocent Africans that we felt it our duty to
make preparations as a long-term undertaking
to use force in order to defend ourselves against
force. If war were inevitable, we wanted the fight
to be conducted on terms most favourable to
our people...

All whites undergo compulsory military training,
but no such training was given to Africans. It was
in our view essential to build up a nucleus of
trained men who would be able to provide the
leadership which would be required if guerrilla
warfare started. We had to prepare for such a
situation before it became too late to make proper
preparations. It was also necessary to build up
a nucleus of men trained in civil administration

and other professions, so that Africans would be
equipped to participate in the government of this
country as soon as they were allowed to do so.

At this stage it was decided that I should attend
the Conference of the Pan-African Freedom
Movement for Central, East, and Southern
Africa, which was to be held early in 1962 in
Addis Ababa, and, because of our need for
preparation, it was also decided that, after the
conference, I would undertake a tour of the
African states with a view to obtaining facilities
for the training of soldiers, and that I would
also solicit scholarships for the higher education
of matriculated Africans. Training in both fields
would be necessary, even if changes came about
by peaceful means...

It was on this note that I left South Africa to
proceed to Addis Ababa as a delegate of the ANC.
My tour was a success. Wherever I went I met
sympathy for our cause and promises of help...

I started to make a study of the art of war and
revolution and, whilst abroad, underwent a course
in military training. If there was to be guerrilla
warfare, I wanted to be able to stand and fight
with my people and to share the hazards of war
with them...

I also made arrangements for our recruits to
undergo military training. But here it was
impossible to organize any scheme without
the cooperation of the ANC offices in Africa.
I consequently obtained the permission of the

ANC in South Africa to do this. To this extent then there was a departure from the original decision of the ANC, but it applied outside South Africa only...

...On my return I found that there had been little alteration in the political scene save that the threat of a death penalty for sabotage had now become a fact...

I wish now to turn to certain general allegations made in this case by the State...

One of the chief allegations in the indictment is that the ANC was a party to a general conspiracy to commit sabotage. I have already explained why this is incorrect but how, externally, there was a departure from the original principle laid down by the ANC... The ANC remained a mass political body of Africans only carrying on the type of political work they had conducted prior to 1961.

Umkhonto remained a small organization recruiting its members from different races and organizations and trying to achieve its own particular object. The fact that members of *Umkhonto* were recruited from the ANC, and the fact that persons served both organizations... did not, in our view, change the nature of the ANC or give it a policy of violence. This overlapping of officers, however, was more the exception than the rule...

Another of the allegations made by the State is that the aims and objects of the ANC and the Communist Party are the same. I wish to deal

with this and with my own political position,
because I must assume that the State may try
to argue from certain Exhibits that I tried to
introduce Marxism into the ANC...

The ideological creed of the ANC is, and always
has been, the creed of African Nationalism. It is
not the concept of African Nationalism expressed
in the cry, '*Drive the White man into the sea*'. The
African Nationalism for which the ANC stands
is the concept of freedom and fulfilment for the
African people in their own land. The most
important political document ever adopted by
the ANC is the 'Freedom Charter'. It is by no
means a blueprint for a socialist state. It calls for
redistribution, but not nationalization, of land;
it provides for nationalization of mines, banks,
and monopoly industry, because big monopolies
are owned by one race only, and without such
nationalization racial domination would be
perpetuated despite the spread of political power.
It would be a hollow gesture to repeal the Gold
Law prohibitions against Africans when all gold
mines are owned by European companies. In this
respect the ANC's policy corresponds with the
old policy of the present Nationalist Party which,
for many years, had as part of its programme the
nationalization of the gold mines which, at that
time, were controlled by foreign capital. Under
the Freedom Charter, nationalization would take
place in an economy based on private enterprise.
The realization of the Freedom Charter would
open up fresh fields for a prosperous African
population of all classes, including the middle
class. The ANC has never at any period of its

history advocated a revolutionary change in the economic structure of the country, nor has it, to the best of my recollection, ever condemned capitalist society.

As far as the Communist Party is concerned, and if I understand its policy correctly, it stands for the establishment of a State based on the principles of Marxism. Although it is prepared to work for the Freedom Charter, as a short-term solution to the problems created by white supremacy, it regards the Freedom Charter as the beginning, and not the end, of its programme.

The ANC, unlike the Communist Party, admitted Africans only as members. Its chief goal was, and is, for the African people to win unity and full political rights. The Communist Party's main aim, on the other hand, was to remove the capitalists and to replace them with a working-class government. The Communist Party sought to emphasize class distinctions whilst the ANC seeks to harmonize them. This is a vital distinction.

It is true that there has often been close cooperation between the ANC and the Communist Party. But cooperation is merely proof of a common goal – in this case the removal of white supremacy – and is not proof of a complete community of interests.

The history of the world is full of similar examples. Perhaps the most striking illustration is to be found in the cooperation between Great Britain, the United States of America, and the Soviet Union in the fight against [Adolf]

Hitler [German dictator, 1933–45]. Nobody
but Hitler would have dared to suggest that
such cooperation turned [Winston] Churchill
or [Franklin D.] Roosevelt [U.S. president,
1933–45] into communists or communist tools,
or that Britain and America were working to
bring about a communist world…

… It is perhaps difficult for white South Africans,
with an ingrained prejudice against communism,
to understand why experienced African politicians
so readily accept communists as their friends. But
to us the reason is obvious. Theoretical differences
amongst those fighting against oppression is a
luxury we cannot afford at this stage. What is
more, for many decades communists were the
only political group in South Africa who were
prepared to treat Africans as human beings and
their equals; who were prepared to eat with us;
talk with us, live with us, and work with us. They
were the only political group which was prepared
to work with the Africans for the attainment of
political rights and a stake in society. Because
of this, there are many Africans who, today, tend
to equate freedom with communism. They are
supported in this belief by a legislature which
brands all exponents of democratic government
and African freedom as communists and bans
many of them (who are not communists) under
the Suppression of Communism Act. Although I
have never been a member of the Communist
Party, I myself have been named under that
pernicious Act because of the role I played in
the Defiance Campaign. I have also been banned
and imprisoned under that Act.

It is not only in internal politics that we count
communists as amongst those who support our
cause. In the international field, communist
countries have always come to our aid. In the
United Nations and other Councils of the world
the communist bloc has supported the Afro-Asian
struggle against colonialism and often seems to
be more sympathetic to our plight than some of
the Western powers. Although there is a universal
condemnation of apartheid, the communist bloc
speaks out against it with a louder voice than most
of the white world...

... I have always regarded myself, in the first
place, as an African patriot. After all, I was born
in Umtata, 46 years ago. My guardian was my
cousin, who was the acting paramount chief of
Tembuland, and I am related both to the present
paramount chief of Tembuland, Sabata Dalindyebo,
and to Kaizer Matanzima, the Chief Minister of
the Transkei.

Today I am attracted by the idea of a classless
society, an attraction which springs in part from
Marxist reading and, in part, from my admiration
of the structure and organization of early African
societies in this country. The land, then the main
means of production, belonged to the tribe. There
were no rich or poor and there was no exploitation.
It is true, as I have already stated, that I have been
influenced by Marxist thought. But this is also true
of many of the leaders of the new independent
States. Such widely different persons as Gandhi,
[Jawaharlal] Nehru [first prime minister of
independent India, 1947–64], Nkrumah, and

[Gamal Abdel] Nasser [president of Egypt, 1956–70]
all acknowledge this fact. We all accept the need for
some form of socialism to enable our people to
catch up with the advanced countries of this world
and to overcome their legacy of extreme poverty.
But this does not mean we are Marxists.

Indeed, for my own part, I believe that it is open
to debate whether the Communist Party has any
specific role to play at this particular stage of our
political struggle. The basic task at the present
moment is the removal of race discrimination
and the attainment of democratic rights on the
basis of the Freedom Charter. In so far as that
Party furthers this task, I welcome its assistance.
I realize that it is one of the means by which
people of all races can be drawn into our struggle.

From my reading of Marxist literature and
from conversations with Marxists, I have gained
the impression that communists regard the
parliamentary system of the West as undemocratic
and reactionary. But, on the contrary, I am an
admirer of such a system.

The Magna Carta [England, 1215], the Petition
of Rights [England, 1628], and the Bill of Rights
[United States, 1791] are documents which are
held in veneration by democrats throughout
the world.

I have great respect for British political institutions,
and for the country's system of justice. I regard
the British Parliament as the most democratic
institution in the world, and the independence

and impartiality of its judiciary never fail to arouse my admiration.

The American Congress, that country's doctrine of separation of powers, as well as the independence of its judiciary, arouses in me similar sentiments.

I have been influenced in my thinking by both West and East. All this has led me to feel that in my search for a political formula, I should be absolutely impartial and objective. I should tie myself to no particular system of society other than of socialism…

As I understand the State case…the suggestion is that *Umkhonto* was the inspiration of the Communist Party which sought by playing upon imaginary grievances to enrol the African people into an army which ostensibly was to fight for African freedom, but in reality was fighting for a communist state. Nothing could be further from the truth. In fact the suggestion is preposterous. *Umkhonto* was formed by Africans to further their struggle for freedom in their own land. Communists and others supported the movement, and we only wish that more sections of the community would join us.

Our fight is against real, and not imaginary, hardships or, to use the language of the State Prosecutor [Percy Yutar, 1911–2002], '*so-called hardships*'. Basically, we fight against two features which are the hallmarks of African life in South Africa and which are entrenched by legislation which we seek to have repealed. These features

are poverty and lack of human dignity, and we
do not need communists or so-called 'agitators'
to teach us about these things.

South Africa is the richest country in Africa,
and could be one of the richest countries in the
world. But it is a land of extremes and remarkable
contrasts. The whites enjoy what may well be
the highest standard of living in the world, whilst
Africans live in poverty and misery. Forty percent
of the Africans live in hopelessly overcrowded and,
in some cases, drought-stricken Reserves, where
soil erosion and the overworking of the soil makes
it impossible for them to live properly off the land.
Thirty percent are labourers, labour tenants, and
squatters on white farms and work and live under
conditions similar to those of the serfs of the
Middle Ages. The other 30 percent live in towns
where they have developed economic and social
habits which bring them closer in many respects
to white standards. Yet most Africans, even in this
group, are impoverished by low incomes and high
cost of living.

The highest-paid and the most prosperous section of
urban African life is in Johannesburg. Yet their actual
position is desperate. The latest figures were given
on 25 March 1964 by Mr Carr, Manager of the
Johannesburg Non-European Affairs Department.
The poverty datum line for the average African
family in Johannesburg (according to M. Carr's
department) is R42.84 per month. He showed
that the average monthly wage is R32.24 and that
46 percent of all African families in Johannesburg
do not earn enough to keep them going.

Poverty goes hand in hand with malnutrition
and disease. The incidence of malnutrition and
deficiency diseases is very high amongst Africans.
Tuberculosis, pellagra, kwashiorkor, gastro-enteritis,
and scurvy bring death and destruction of health.
The incidence of infant mortality is one of the
highest in the world. According to the Medical
Officer of Health for Pretoria, tuberculosis kills
40 people a day (almost all Africans), and in
1961 there were 58,491 new cases reported.
These diseases not only destroy the vital organs
of the body, but they result in retarded mental
conditions and lack of initiative, and reduce powers
of concentration. The secondary results of such
conditions affect the whole community and the
standard of work performed by African labourers.

The complaint of Africans, however, is not only that
they are poor and the whites are rich, but that the
laws which are made by the whites are designed to
preserve this situation. There are two ways to break
out of poverty. The first is by formal education, and
the second is by the worker acquiring a greater skill
at his work and thus higher wages. As far as Africans
are concerned, both these avenues of advancement
are deliberately curtailed by legislation.

The present Government has always sought to
hamper Africans in their search for education.
One of their early acts, after coming into power,
was to stop subsidies for African school feeding.
Many African children who attended schools
depended on this supplement to their diet. This
was a cruel act.

There is compulsory education for all white
children at virtually no cost to their parents,
be they rich or poor. Similar facilities are not
provided for the African children, though there
are some who receive such assistance. African
children, however, generally have to pay more
for their schooling than whites…

The quality of education is also different… This
is presumably consistent with the policy of Bantu
education about which the present Prime Minister
[Hendrik Verwoerd, in office 1958–66] said, during
the debate on the Bantu Education Bill in 1953:

> '*When I have control of Native education I will
> reform it so that Natives will be taught from
> childhood to realise that equality with Europeans
> is not for them…. People who believe in equality
> are not desirable teachers for Natives*'.

The other main obstacle to the economic
advancement of the African is the industrial
colour-bar under which all the better jobs of
industry are reserved for Whites only. Moreover,
Africans who do obtain employment in the
unskilled and semi-skilled occupations which
are open to them are not allowed to form
trade unions which have recognition under the
Industrial Conciliation Act. This means that strikes
of African workers are illegal, and that they are
denied the right of collective bargaining which
is permitted to the better-paid White workers.
The discrimination in the policy of successive
South African Governments towards African
workers is demonstrated by the so-called 'civilized

labour policy' under which sheltered, unskilled Government jobs are found for those white workers who cannot make the grade in industry, at wages which far exceed the earnings of the average African employee in industry.

The Government often answers its critics by saying that Africans in South Africa are economically better off than the inhabitants of the other countries in Africa. I do not know whether this statement is true and doubt whether any comparison can be made without having regard to the cost-of-living index in such countries. But even if it is true, as far as the African people are concerned it is irrelevant. Our complaint is not that we are poor by comparison with people in other countries, but that we are poor by comparison with the white people in our own country, and that we are prevented by legislation from altering this imbalance.

The lack of human dignity experienced by Africans is the direct result of the policy of white supremacy. White supremacy implies black inferiority. Legislation designed to preserve white supremacy entrenches this notion. Menial tasks in South Africa are invariably performed by Africans. When anything has to be carried or cleaned the white man will look around for an African to do it for him, whether the African is employed by him or not. Because of this sort of attitude, whites tend to regard Africans as a separate breed. They do not look upon them as people with families of their own; they do not realise that they have emotions – that they fall in love like white people do; that they want to be with their wives and children like white people want to be with theirs; that they want to earn enough money to support their families properly, to feed and clothe them and send them to school. And what 'house-boy' or 'garden-boy' or labourer can ever hope to do this?

Pass laws, which to the Africans are among the most hated bits of legislation in South Africa, render any African liable to police surveillance at any time. I doubt whether there is a single African male in South Africa who has not at some stage had a brush with the police over his pass. Hundreds and thousands of Africans are thrown into jail each year under pass laws. Even worse than this is the fact that pass laws keep husband and wife apart and lead to the breakdown of family life.

Poverty and the breakdown of family life have secondary effects. Children wander about the streets of the townships because they have no schools to go to, or no money to enable them to go to school, or no parents at home to see that they go to school, because both parents (if there be two) have to work to keep the family alive. This leads to a breakdown in moral standards, to an alarming rise in illegitimacy, and to growing violence which erupts not only politically, but everywhere. Life in the townships is dangerous. There is not a day that goes by without somebody being stabbed or assaulted. And violence is carried out of the townships in the white living areas. People are afraid to walk alone in the streets after dark. Housebreakings and robberies are increasing, despite the fact that the death sentence can now be imposed for such offences. Death sentences cannot cure the festering sore.

Africans want to be paid a living wage.

Africans want to perform work which they are capable of doing, and not work which the Government declares them to be capable of. Africans want to be allowed to live where they obtain work, and not be endorsed out of an area because they were not born there.

Africans want to be allowed to own land in places where they work, and not to be obliged to live in rented houses which they can never call their own.

Africans want to be part of the general population, and not confined to living in their own ghettoes. African men want to have their wives and children to live with them where they work, and not be forced into an unnatural existence in men's hostels. African women want to be with their menfolk and not be left permanently widowed in the Reserves.

Africans want to be allowed out after eleven o'clock at night and not to be confined to their rooms like little children.

Africans want to be allowed to travel in their own country and to seek work where they want to and not where the Labour Bureau tells them to.

Africans want a just share in the whole of South Africa; they want security and a stake in society.

Above all, we want equal political rights, because
without them our disabilities will be permanent.
I know this sounds revolutionary to the whites
in this country, because the majority of voters
will be Africans. This makes the white man
fear democracy.

But this fear cannot be allowed to stand in the
way of the only solution which will guarantee
racial harmony and freedom for all. It is not true
that the enfranchisement of all will result in racial
domination. Political division, based on colour, is
entirely artificial and, when it disappears, so will
the domination of one colour group by another.
The ANC has spent half a century fighting against
racialism. When it triumphs it will not change
that policy.

This then is what the ANC is fighting. Their
struggle is a truly national one. It is a struggle of
the African people, inspired by their own suffering
and their own experience. It is a struggle for the
right to live.

During my lifetime I have dedicated myself to
this struggle of the African people. I have fought
against white domination, and I have fought
against black domination. I have cherished the
ideal of a democratic and free society in which
all persons live together in harmony and with
equal opportunities. It is an ideal which I hope
to live for and to achieve. But if needs be, it is
an ideal for which I am prepared to die.

Temptations and Traps
Pollsmoor Prison, 10 February 1985

It was almost inevitable that Mandela would be found guilty. The verdict was handed down on 11 June 1964 and Judge Quartus de Wet (1899–1980) adjourned the court until the following morning to complete his deliberations. On 12 June Mandela was sentenced to life imprisonment along with seven of his co-defendants – Walter Sisulu, Govan Mbeki (1910–2001; ANC national chairman), Raymond Mhlaba (1920–2005), Elias Motsoaledi (1924–94), Andrew Mlangeni (b. 1926), Ahmed Kathrada (b. 1929) and Denis Goldberg (b. 1933).

Although cut off from the world in prison, Mandela remained a thorn in the side of the apartheid regime. He had too much support both at home and abroad to be eliminated, the fate that befell other opponents of apartheid, most famously Steve Biko (1946–77), the founder of the Black Consciousness Movement, who died after being severely beaten in police custody. From time to time the government offered Mandela his freedom on condition that he went to live quietly in the Transkei bantustan. Mandela refused on the grounds that the bantustans – 10 territories designated as homelands for the country's black Africans – were a sham.

Then, unexpectedly, on 31 January 1985, P.W. (Pieter Willem) Botha (1916–2006; president of South Africa 1984–9) announced during a debate in the national parliament that he would free

Mandela on condition that he '*unconditionally rejected violence as a political weapon*', adding: '*It is therefore not the South African government which now stands in the way of Mr Mandela's freedom. It is he himself*'.

Mandela recognized that the offer was an attempt to drive a wedge between him and his ANC colleagues, particularly Oliver Tambo, who had gone into exile in 1960 and later settled in Zambia, where he set up the foreign headquarters of the ANC and became its leader in 1969.

Mandela prepared a careful response which was read on his behalf by his daughter, Zindzi (b. 1960), at a mass meeting in Jabulani Stadium, Soweto, on 10 February 1985. By invoking the names of three former prime ministers of South Africa, with whom he had previously tried to negotiate, he displays not only his knowledge of history but also his part in it.

I am a member of the African National Congress. I have always been a member of the African National Congress and I will remain a member of the African National Congress until the day I die. Oliver Tambo is much more than a brother to me. He is my greatest friend and comrade for nearly fifty years. If there is any one amongst you who cherishes my freedom, Oliver Tambo cherishes it more, and I know that he would give his life to see me free. There is no difference between his views and mine.

I am surprised at the conditions that the government wants to impose on me. I am not a violent man. My colleagues and I wrote in 1952 to [Daniel F.] Malan [1874–1959; prime minister of South Africa 1948–59] asking for a round table conference to find a solution to the problems of our country, but that was ignored. When [Johannes Gerhardus] Strijdom [1893–1958; prime minister of South Africa 1954–8] was in power, we made the same offer. Again it was ignored. When [Hendrik] Verwoerd [1901–66; prime minister of South Africa 1958–66] was in power we asked for a national convention for all the people in South Africa to decide on their future. This, too, was in vain.

It was only then, when all other forms of resistance were no longer open to us, that we turned to armed struggle. Let Botha show that he is different to Malan, Strijdom and Verwoerd. Let him renounce violence. Let him say that he will dismantle apartheid. Let him unban the people's organization, the African National Congress. Let him free all who have been imprisoned, banished or exiled for their opposition to apartheid. Let him guarantee free political activity so that people may decide who will govern them.

I cherish my own freedom dearly, but I care even more for your freedom [that of the audience]. Too many have died since I went to prison. Too many have suffered for the love of freedom. I owe it to their widows, to their orphans, to their mothers and to their fathers who have grieved and wept for them. Not only I have suffered during these long, lonely, wasted years. I am not less life-loving than you are. But I cannot sell my birthright, nor

am I prepared to sell the birthright of the people
to be free. I am in prison as the representative of
the people and of your organization, the African
National Congress, which was banned.

What freedom am I being offered while the
organization of the people remains banned?
What freedom am I being offered when I
may be arrested on a pass offence? What
freedom am I being offered to live my life as
a family with my dear wife who remains in
banishment in Brandfort [a town in the Free
State Province – then the Orange Free State –
where Winnie Mandela had been exiled since
her release in 1977 after serving six months in
jail for her part in the 1976 Soweto Uprising]?
What freedom am I being offered when I
must ask for permission to live in an urban
area? What freedom am I being offered when
I need a stamp in my pass to seek work? What
freedom am I being offered when my very
South African citizenship is not respected?

Only free men can negotiate. Prisoners cannot
enter into contracts…

I cannot and will not give any undertaking at a
time when I and you, the people, are not free.

Your freedom and mine cannot be separated. I
will return.

Meeting with Botha

Tuynhuys, Cape Town, 5 July 1989

International pressure on the apartheid regime increased and, in the early months of 1989, Mandela was informed that Botha was prepared to meet him in person. Mandela prepared a written statement to the South African president in which he outlined his concerns. The most important of these was that the author was not, and should not be regarded as, a representative of or spokesman for the elected leadership of the ANC; he was merely a facilitator who would help to clarify the organization's policies in certain areas if asked to do so. The statement is a masterfully succinct résumé of both the ANC's position and his own, again emphasizing that the ANC has been forced to take action and abandon its original non-violent stance due to the 'violent' action against the black population under apartheid. Note particularly Mandela's anxiety that any discussions should be about the movement as a whole rather than his own imprisonment.

The deepening political crisis in our country has been a matter of grave concern to me for quite some time and I now consider it necessary in the national interest for the African National Congress and the government to meet urgently to negotiate an effective political settlement.

At the outset I must point out that I make this move without consultation with the ANC. I am a loyal and disciplined member of the ANC, my political loyalty is owed, primarily, if not exclusively, to this organization and particularly to our Lusaka [Zambia] headquarters where the official leadership is stationed and from where our affairs are directed...

I must further point out that the question of my release from prison is not an issue, at least at this stage of the discussions, and I am certainly not asking to be freed. But I do hope that the government will, as soon as possible, give me the opportunity from my present quarters to sound the views of my colleagues inside and outside the country on this move. Only if this initiative is formally endorsed by the ANC will it have any significance...

The position of the ANC on the question of violence is very simple. The organization has no vested interest in violence. It abhors any action which may cause loss of life, destruction of property and misery to the people. It has worked long and patiently for a South Africa of common values and for an undivided and peaceful non-racial state. But we consider the armed struggle a legitimate form of self-defence against a morally repugnant system of government which will not allow even peaceful forms of protest.

It is more than ironical that it should be the government which demands that we should renounce violence. The government knows only too well that there is not a single political organization in this country, inside and outside

parliament, which can ever compare with the
ANC in its total commitment to peaceful change.

Right from the early days of its history, the
organization diligently sought peaceful solutions
and, to that extent, it talked patiently to successive
South African governments, a policy we tried to
follow in dealing with the present government...

Not only did the government ignore our demands
for a meeting, instead it took advantage of our
commitment to a non-violent struggle and
unleashed the most violent form of racial
oppression this country has ever seen. It stripped
us of all basic human rights, outlawed our
organizations and barred all channels of peaceful
resistance. It met our demands with force and,
despite the grave problems facing the country,
it continues to refuse to talk to us. There can
only be one answer to this challenge; violent
forms of struggle.

Down the years oppressed people have fought
for their birthright by peaceful means, where that
was possible, and through force where peaceful
channels were closed. The history of this country
also confirms this vital lesson. Africans as well as
Afrikaners were, at one time or other, compelled
to take up arms in defence of their freedom against
British imperialism. The fact that both were finally
defeated by superior arms, and by the vast resources
of that empire, does not negate this lesson.

But from what has happened in South Africa
during the last 40 years, we must conclude that

now that the roles are reversed, and the Afrikaner
is no longer a freedom fighter, but is in power,
the entire lesson of history must be brushed
aside. Not even a disciplined non-violent protest
will now be tolerated. To the government a
black man has neither a just cause to espouse
nor freedom rights to defend. The whites
must have the monopoly of political power,
and of committing violence against innocent
and defenceless people. That situation was
totally unacceptable to us and the formation
of Umkhonto we Sizwe was intended to end
that monopoly, and to forcibly bring home to
the government that the oppressed people of
this country were prepared to stand up and
defend themselves.

It is significant to note that throughout the past
four decades, and more especially over the last 26
years, the government has met our demands with
force only and has done hardly anything to create
a suitable climate for dialogue. On the contrary,
the government continues to govern with a heavy
hand, and to incite whites against negotiation
with the ANC...

The truth is that the government is not yet ready
for negotiation and for the sharing of political
power with blacks. It is still committed to white
domination and, for that reason, it will only
tolerate those blacks who are willing to serve on its
apartheid structures. Its policy is to remove from the
political scene blacks who refuse to conform, who
reject white supremacy and its apartheid structures,
and who insist on equal rights with whites.

This is the real reason for the government's refusal to talk to us, and for its demand that we should disarm ourselves, while it continues to use violence against our people. This is the reason for its massive propaganda campaign to discredit the ANC, and present it to the public as a communist-dominated organization bent on murder and destruction. In this situation the reaction of the oppressed people is clearly predictable...

White South Africa must accept the plain fact that the ANC will not suspend, to say nothing of abandoning, the armed struggle until the government shows its willingness to surrender the monopoly of political power, and to negotiate directly and in good faith with the acknowledged black leaders. The renunciation of violence by either the government or the ANC should not be a precondition to, but the result of, negotiation...

We equally reject the charge that the ANC is dominated by the SACP [South African Communist Party] and we regard the accusation as part of the smear campaign the government is waging against us...

The government also accuses us of being agents of the Soviet Union. The truth is that the ANC is non-aligned, and we welcome support from the East and the West, from the socialist and capitalist countries. The only difference... is that the socialist countries supply us with weapons, which the West refuses to give us. We have no intention whatsoever of changing our stand on this question.

The government's exaggerated hostility to the
SACP and its refusal to have any dealings with
that party have a hollow ring. Such an attitude
is not only out of step with the growing
cooperation between the capitalist and socialist
countries in different parts of the world, but
it is also inconsistent with the policy of the
government itself, when dealing with our
neighbouring states.

Not only has South Africa concluded treaties with
the Marxist states of Angola and Mozambique –
quite rightly in our opinion – but she also wants
to strengthen ties with Marxist Zimbabwe. The
government will certainly find it difficult, if
not altogether impossible, to reconcile its
readiness to work with foreign Marxists for
the peaceful resolution of mutual problems,
with its uncompromising refusal to talk to
South African Marxists.

The reason for this inconsistency is obvious. As
I have already said, the government is still too
deeply committed to the principle of white
domination and, despite lip service to reform,
it is deadly opposed to the sharing of political
power with blacks, and the SACP is merely being
used as a smokescreen to retain the monopoly of
political power.

The smear campaign against the ANC also helps
the government to evade the real issue at stake,
namely, the exclusion from political power of the
black majority by a white minority, which is the
source of all our troubles

It is true... that I have been influenced by
Marxist thought. But this is also true of many
leaders of the new independent states. Such
widely different persons as Gandhi, Nehru,
Nkrumah and Nasser all acknowledge this
fact. We all accept the need for some form
of socialism to enable our people to catch
up with the advanced countries of the world,
and to overcome their legacy of poverty...

The government is equally vehement in
condemning the principle of majority rule...
Yet majority rule and internal peace are like
the two sides of a single coin, and white
South Africa simply has to accept that there
will never be peace and stability in this
country until the principle is fully applied.

It is precisely because of its denial that the
government has become the enemy of practically
every black man. It is that denial that has sparked
off the current civil strife...

By insisting on compliance with the above-
mentioned conditions before there can be talks,
the government clearly confirms that it wants
no peace in this country but turmoil...

No worthy leaders of a freedom movement
will ever submit to conditions which are
essentially terms of surrender dictated by a
victorious commander to a beaten enemy,
and which are really intended to weaken the
organization and to humiliate its leadership.

The key to the whole situation is a negotiated settlement, and a meeting between the government and the ANC will be the first major step towards lasting peace in the country...

I believe that the overwhelming majority of South Africans, black and white, hope to see the ANC and the government working closely together to lay the foundations for a new era in our country, in which racial discrimination and prejudice, coercion and confrontation death and destruction will be forgotten.

Chapter 3
Release and Triumph
(1990–94)

During the next phase of his life, Nelson Mandela went from the extraordinary position of prisoner to president. At the start of it he was known as 'No. 46664'; at the end of it he was '*Madiba*', the respectful form of address to members of his clan. Many people thought that the transition would be unendurably traumatic for a man in his 70s but, after an uncertain start, Mandela rose to new heights and revelled in his triple role as politician, statesman and, much to his surprise and delight, superstar. The rapid ascent is well reflected in his speeches of this period, which begin with an understandably hesitant performance on the day of his release and end with the triumph of his inauguration.

On 2 February 1990, F.W. de Klerk (b. 1936), who succeeded P.W. Botha as President of South Africa in September 1989, lifted the ban on the ANC and other proscribed opposition organizations and thus commenced the dismantling of apartheid. At a meeting eight days later, de Klerk and Mandela agreed that the latter would be released the following afternoon.

Mandela and his advisers gave much thought to how and where he should spend the night of his release: this was not just the end of one man's sentence; it was the start of a new chapter in the history of a nation.

At 3.30 p.m. on 11 February 1990, after 27½ years – 10,000 days – in jail, Nelson Mandela walked out of the front gates of Victor Verster Prison (now Drakenstein Correctional Centre) in Paarl, Western Cape Province. His wife, Winnie, was with him.

Into the Light

City Hall, Cape Town, 11 February 1990

From jail, Mandela was driven 40 miles (64 km) to Cape Town, where he made a speech from a balcony of City Hall. This was the first time he had spoken directly to all the people of South Africa. While he had been quite unprepared for the number of people in the audience – there was an estimated crowd of 50,000, and the speech was broadcast by radio and television around the world – he had had ample time to choose his words with even greater than usual care. After thanking those who helped him during his long imprisonment – a rhetorically formal introduction in which he uses the words '*I salute*' eight times and '*I pay tribute*' three times – he moves directly to a peroration that includes, in quick succession, two uses of the word '*democracy*', four of '*democratic*' and one of '*democratically*'. These repetitions are a deliberate strategy to get the key message across, then consolidate and reaffirm it. It also palliates the more combative phrases – '*mass action*' and '*armed struggle*' – which might have alarmed mainstream opinion. Finally, Mandela harks back to the Rivonia Trial (see pages 32–62), thereby emphasizing his own part in South Africa's progression towards the end of apartheid. This speech is also the first in which Mandela says that he is not a 'prophet' – a phrase that he had cause to use again repeatedly over the coming years.

Friends, comrades and fellow South Africans,

I greet you all in the name of peace, democracy and freedom for all.

I stand here before you not as a prophet but as a humble servant of you, the people. Your tireless and heroic sacrifices have made it possible for me to be here today. I therefore place the remaining years of my life in your hands.

On this day of my release, I extend my sincere and warmest gratitude to the millions of my compatriots and those in every corner of the globe who have campaigned tirelessly for my release.

I send special greetings to the people of Cape Town, this city which has been my home for three decades. Your mass marches and other forms of struggle have served as a constant source of strength to all political prisoners.

I salute the African National Congress. It has fulfilled our every expectation in its role as leader of the great march to freedom.

I salute our President, Comrade Oliver Tambo, for leading the ANC even under the most difficult circumstances.

I salute the rank and file members of the ANC. You have sacrificed life and limb in the pursuit of the noble cause of our struggle.

I salute combatants of *Umkhonto we Sizwe*, like Solomon Mahlangu [1956–79; member of MK, executed in 1979] and Ashley Kriel [1966–87; student activist killed by security police] who have paid the ultimate price for the freedom of all South Africans.

I salute the South African Communist Party for its sterling contribution to the struggle for democracy. You have survived 40 years of unrelenting persecution…

I salute General Secretary Joe Slovo, one of our finest patriots. We are heartened by the fact that the alliance between ourselves and the Party remains as strong as it always was.

I salute the United Democratic Front, the National Education Crisis Committee, the South African Youth Congress, the Transvaal and Natal Indian Congresses and COSATU [Congress of South African Trade Unions] and the many other formations of the Mass Democratic Movement.

I also salute the Black Sash [non-violent white women's resistance organization] and the National Union of South African Students. We note with pride that you have acted as the conscience of white South Africa. Even during the darkest days in the history of our struggle you held the flag of liberty high. The large-scale mass mobilization of the past few years is one of the key factors which led to the opening of the final chapter of our struggle.

I extend my greetings to the working class of our country. Your organized strength is the pride of our movement. You remain the most dependable force in the struggle to end exploitation and oppression.

I pay tribute to the many religious communities who carried the campaign for justice forward when the organizations for our people were silenced...

I pay tribute to the endless heroism of youth, you, the young lions. You, the young lions, have energized our entire struggle.

I pay tribute to the mothers and wives and sisters of our nation. You are the rock-hard foundation of our struggle. Apartheid has inflicted more pain on you than on anyone else.

On this occasion we thank the world community for their great contribution to the anti-apartheid struggle. Without your support our struggle would not have reached this advanced stage. The sacrifice of the frontline states will be remembered by South Africans forever. My salutations would be incomplete without expressing my deep appreciation for the strength given to me during my long and lonely years in prison by my beloved wife and family. I am convinced that your pain and suffering was far greater than my own...

Today the majority of South Africans, black and white, recognize that apartheid has no future. It has to be ended by our own decisive mass action in order to build peace and security. The mass campaign of defiance and other actions of our organization and people can only culminate in the establishment of democracy. The destruction caused by apartheid on our sub-continent is incalculable. The fabric of family life of millions of my people has been shattered. Millions are homeless and unemployed. Our economy lies in ruins and our people are embroiled in political strife. Our resort to the armed struggle in 1960 with the formation of the military wing of the ANC, Umkhonto we Sizwe, was a purely defensive action against the violence of apartheid. The factors which necessitated the armed struggle still exist today. We have no option but to continue. We express the hope that a climate conducive to a negotiated settlement will be created soon so that there may no longer be the need for the armed struggle. I am a loyal and disciplined member of the African National Congress. I am therefore in full agreement with all of its objectives, strategies and tactics.

The need to unite the people of our country is as important a task now as it always has been. No individual leader is able to take on this enormous task on his own. It is our task as leaders to place our views before our organization and to allow the democratic structures to decide. On the question of democratic practice, I feel duty bound to make the point that a leader of the movement is a person who has been democratically elected at a national conference. This is a principle which must be upheld without any exceptions.

Today, I wish to report to you that my talks with the government have been aimed at normalizing the political situation in the country. We have not as yet begun discussing the basic demands of the struggle. I wish to stress that I myself have at no time entered into negotiations about the future of our country except to insist on a meeting between the ANC and the government.

Mr de Klerk has gone further than any other Nationalist president in taking real steps to normalize the situation. However, there are further steps... that have to be met before negotiations on the basic demands of our people can begin. I reiterate our call for, inter alia, the immediate ending of the State of Emergency and the freeing of all, and not only some, political prisoners. Only such a normalized situation, which allows for free political activity, can allow us to consult our people in order to obtain a mandate.

The people need to be consulted on who will negotiate and on the content of such negotiations. Negotiations cannot take place above the heads or behind the backs of our people. It is our belief that the future of our country can only be determined by a body which is democratically

elected on a non-racial basis... There must be
an end to white monopoly on political power
and a fundamental restructuring of our political
and economic systems to ensure that the
inequalities of apartheid are addressed and our
society thoroughly democratized.

It must be added that Mr de Klerk himself is a man
of integrity who is acutely aware of the dangers of a
public figure not honouring his undertakings. But as
an organization we base our policy and strategy on
the harsh reality we are faced with. And this reality
is that we are still suffering under the policy of the
Nationalist government.

Our struggle has reached a decisive moment.
We call on our people to seize this moment so
that the process towards democracy is rapid and
uninterrupted. We have waited too long for our
freedom. We can no longer wait. Now is the time
to intensify the struggle on all fronts. To relax our
efforts now would be a mistake which generations
to come will not be able to forgive. The sight of
freedom looming on the horizon should
encourage us to redouble our efforts.

It is only through disciplined mass action that our
victory can be assured. We call on our white
compatriots to join us in the shaping of a new
South Africa. The freedom movement is a political
home for you too. We call on the international
community to continue the campaign to isolate
the apartheid regime. To lift sanctions now would
be to run the risk of aborting the process towards
the complete eradication of apartheid.

Our march to freedom is irreversible. We must not allow fear to stand in our way. Universal suffrage on a common voters' role in a united democratic and non-racial South Africa is the only way to peace and racial harmony.

In conclusion I wish to quote my own words during my trial in 1964. They are true today as they were then:

> *I have fought against white domination and I have fought against black domination. I have cherished the ideal of a democratic and free society in which all persons live together in harmony and with equal opportunities. It is an ideal which I hope to live for and to achieve. But if needs be, it is an ideal for which I am prepared to die.*

Return to London
Wembley Stadium, 16 April 1990

Over the next six months, Mandela spent more time abroad than in South Africa, as he visited world leaders to attract support and sponsorship for the ANC struggle. His gruelling itinerary included two visits to London. On the first of these trips, he turned down an invitation to meet British prime minister Margaret Thatcher – by now, one of the few remaining opponents of sanctions against the apartheid regime – and instead went to a concert in his

**honour at Wembley Stadium, which was attended
by 75,000 people and televised live by the BBC.
At the finale, Mandela strode up and down the
stage with a clenched fist and delivered one of his
best-known speeches.**

Our first simple and happy task is to say thank you.
Thank you very much to you all. Thank you that
you chose to care, because you could have decided
otherwise. Thank you that you elected not to
forget, because our fate could have been a passing
concern. We are here today because for almost
three decades you sustained a campaign for the
unconditional release of all South African political
prisoners. We are here because you took the
humane decision that you could not ignore the
inhumanity represented by the apartheid system.
Even through the thickness of the prison walls at
Robben Island… we heard your voices demanding
our freedom. During all the days we spent buried
in the apartheid dungeons, we never lost our
confidence in the certainty of our release and
our victory over the apartheid system. This was
because we knew that not even the hard-hearted
men of Pretoria [the administrative capital of South
Africa] could withstand the enormous strength
represented by the concerted effort of the peoples
of South Africa and the rest of the world…

We are meeting here to celebrate the victory
represented by the release of some of us. We
must however remember that only a few have
been released. A greater number remains in prison.
We should therefore treat this day of celebration
as one of rededication to the continuation and

intensification of the struggle for the emancipation of all the remaining political prisoners.

We must also view it as a day of renewed commitment to the furtherance of the struggle against the system which keeps those outstanding sons and daughters of our people in jail. Together we must pledge to continue our united offensive for the abolition of the apartheid system.

The apartheid crime against humanity remains in place. It continues to kill and main. It continues to oppress and exploit. Its blood-stained offsprings continue to rain death and destruction on the peoples of Mozambique and Angola. Every day it produces orphans throughout Southern Africa.

Therefore do not listen to anyone who says that you must give up the struggle against apartheid. Reject any suggestion that the campaign to isolate the apartheid system should be wound down. It is only those who support apartheid who can argue that the Pretoria government should be rewarded for the small steps it has taken, such as our release and the unbanning of the ANC and the other organizations.

The reward the people of South Africa, of Southern Africa and the rest of the world seek, is the end of apartheid and the transformation of our country into a non-racial democracy. That prospect will only become reality as a result of struggle, including the struggle represented by the international sanctions campaign. All of us must therefore refuse to be demobilized, even if those who seek to demobilize us plead that they are doing so out of a new-found concern for the oppressed...

Dear friends, it will not be long now before we see the end of the apartheid system. The dreams of millions of people to see our country free nd at peace will be realized sooner rather than later. We are determined to ensure that our country is transformed from being the skunk of the world into an exemplary oasis of unrivalled and excelllent race relations, democracy for all, a just peace and freedom from poverty and human degradation.

Let us continue to march forward together for the realization of that glorious vision. It will be a proud day for all humanity when we are all able to say that the apartheid crime against humanity is no more. Then shall we all converge on the cities, towns and villages of South Africa to celebrate that moment when by ending the system of white minority domination, humanity will have ensured that never again shall the scourge of racial tyranny raise its ugly head.

You will all be welcome to attend those historic victory celebrations… Finally, I want to tell you… that we respect you, we admire you and, above all, we love you!

Flash of Anger

Kempton Park, South Africa, 20 December 1991

Almost all Mandela's mature public speeches have been characterized by the moderation of their tone, language and sentiment. However, one

of the great man's few displays of temper came, in 1991, at the end of the first day of the Convention for a Democratic South Africa (CODESA). After F.W. de Klerk, whose speech was meant to end the day, attacked the ANC for maintaining *Umkhonto we Sizwe*, Mandela made the following biting comments. He refers to the President in the third person and makes it clear that de Klerk's remarks are not just unreasonable, but are also made by someone who sometimes doesn't understand democracy – someone who is a *'product of apartheid'*.

... He has launched an attack on the African National Congress, and in doing so he has been less than frank. Even the head of an illegitimate, discredited minority regime, as his, has certain moral standards to uphold. He has no excuse, because he is a representative of a discredited regime, not to uphold moral standards....

If Mr de Klerk promises to do his duty as the head or Government, to put an end to the violence, to restrain his security services, to clean the country of hit squads and other elements which are responsible for killing innocent people, then he can come to us and say: *I want you to hand over your weapons to us for joint control.* But as long as he's playing this double game, he must be clear that we are not going to co-operate with him on this matter. He can do what he likes. We are not going to disband *Umkhonto we Sizwe.* We are not a political party. We are a political organization, perhaps with more support world-wide than he has. We have used *Umkhonto we Sizwe* to help in the exertion of pressure on the Government to change its policies.

We have no illusions. It is not the operations of
Umkhonto alone which have brought about these
developments, but *Umkhonto* has had a very
significant contribution towards the struggle and
cannot hand over that instrument to the National
Party.... A number of people have paid him
compliments. Very well, we agree with that. He has
tried to undo what his brothers have done to us.
Through the policy of apartheid, they have created
misery beyond words. Nevertheless, we are prepared
to forget and he has made a contribution towards
normalizing the situation because without him we
would not have made this progress...

Let's work together, openly. Let there be no secret
agendas. Let him not persuade us that he should be
the last speaker – because he wants to abuse that
privilege and to attack us in the hope that he will
get no reply.

I am prepared to work with him in spite of all his
mistakes And I am prepared to make allowances
because he is a product of apartheid. Although he
wants these democratic changes, he has sometimes
very little idea what democracy means...

He doesn't represent us. He can't talk to us in
that language, but nevertheless I am prepared to
work with him to see to it that these democratic
changes are introduced in the country and we
can only succeed if we are candid and open with
one another. This type of thing, of trying to take
advantage of the co-operation which we are giving
... willingly, is something extremely dangerous and
I hope this is the last time he will do so...

Nobel Laureate

Oslo, Norway, 10 December 1993

In July 1991, Oliver Tambo stood down as president of the ANC and Mandela was unanimously elected as his successor. South Africa was now moving towards rehabilitation within the global community but domestically the road to democracy was tough, marred by politically related violence.

This was also a period of personal difficulty for Mandela. In 1992, he left Winnie, his wife of 34 years, after she had been sentenced to 6 years in prison for her part in the 1988 kidnapping of 4 black youths, one of whom was murdered by her chief bodyguard.

Against this background, Mandela and de Klerk continued to lay the foundations of a new South Africa. Despite the occasional strain in their relationship, in 1993 Mandela and F.W. de Klerk were jointly awarded the Nobel Peace Prize for their work to bring South Africa from apartheid to democracy.

The following text, Mandela's acceptance speech, demonstrates a strong association with previous laureates, including fellow South Africans Albert Luthuli and Desmond Tutu. Again remarkable are the characteristic vacillations between the first persons singular and plural. Mandela, for all his life unwavering in his belief in the justice of his

struggle, frequently sounds uncertain about the boundaries between his identity as an individual and his role as a representative or figurehead of the ANC. In quoting the words '*the wretched of the earth*' – part of the opening line of the socialist anthem the 'Internationale' – Mandela aligns himself with freedom struggles worldwide.

… I extend my heartfelt thanks to the Norwegian Nobel Committee for elevating us to the status of a Nobel Peace Prize winner. I would also like to take this opportunity to congratulate my compatriot and fellow laureate, State President F.W. de Klerk, on his receipt of this high honour.

Together, we join two distinguished South Africans, the late Chief Albert Luthuli and His Grace Archbishop Desmond Tutu, to whose seminal contributions to the peaceful struggle against the evil system of apartheid you paid well-deserved tribute by awarding them the Nobel Peace Prize.

It will not be presumptuous of us if we also add, among our predecessors, the name of another outstanding Nobel Peace Prize winner, the late Rev. Martin Luther King Jr. …

We speak here of the challenge of the dichotomies of war and peace, violence and non-violence, racism and human dignity, oppression and repression and liberty and human rights, poverty and freedom from want.

We stand here today as nothing more than a representative of the millions of our people who dared to rise up against a social system whose very essence is war, violence, racism, oppression, repression and the impoverishment of an entire people.

I am also here today as a representative of the millions of people across the globe, the anti-apartheid movement, the governments and organizations that joined with us, not to fight against South Africa as a country or any of its peoples, but to oppose an inhuman system and sue for a speedy end to the apartheid crime against humanity.

These countless human beings, both inside and outside our country, had the nobility of spirit to stand in the path of tyranny and injustice, without seeking selfish gain. They recognized that an injury to one is an injury to all and therefore acted together in defence of justice and a common human decency.

Because of their courage and persistence for many years, we can, today, even set the dates when all humanity will join together to celebrate one of the outstanding human victories of our century.

When that moment comes, we shall, together, rejoice in a common victory over racism, apartheid and white minority rule. That triumph will finally bring to a close a history of 500 years of African colonization...

Thus, it will mark a great step forward in history and also serve as a common pledge of the peoples of the world to fight racism, wherever it occurs and whatever guise it assumes...

The value of that gift to all who have suffered will and must be measured by the happiness and welfare

of all the people of our country, who will have
torn down the inhuman walls that divide them.

These great masses will have turned their backs on
the grave insult to human dignity which described
some as masters and others as servants, and
transformed each into a predator whose survival
depended on the destruction of the other.

The value of our shared reward will and must be
measured by the joyful peace which will triumph,
because the common humanity that bonds both
black and white into one human race, will have
said to each one of us that we shall all live like the
children of paradise.

Thus shall we live, because we will have created
a society which recognizes that all people are
born equal, with each entitled in equal measure
to life, liberty, prosperity, human rights and good
governance. Such a society should never allow again
that there should be prisoners of conscience nor
that any person's human right should be violated.
Neither should it ever happen that once more the
avenues to peaceful change are blocked by usurpers
who seek to take power away from the people, in
pursuit of their own, ignoble purposes.

In relation to these matters, we appeal to those who
govern Burma that they release our fellow Nobel
Peace Prize laureate, Aung San Suu Kyi, and engage
her and those she represents in serious dialogue, for
the benefit of all the people of Burma... We do not
believe that this Nobel Peace Prize is intended as a
commendation for matters that have happened and

passed. We hear the voices which say that it is an appeal from all those, throughout the universe, who sought an end to the system of apartheid.

We understand their call, that we devote what remains of our lives to the use of our country's unique and painful experience to demonstrate, in practice, that the normal condition for human existence is democracy, justice, peace, non-racism, non-sexism, prosperity for everybody, a healthy environment and equality and solidarity among the peoples.

Moved by that appeal and inspired by the eminence you have thrust upon us, we undertake that we too will do what we can to contribute to the renewal of our world so that none should, in future, be described as '*the wretched of the earth*'...

Let Freedom Reign

Pretoria, 10 May 1994

After four years' preparation, on 27 and 28 April 1994, South Africa held the first free democratic election in its history. The ANC secured 252 of the 400 seats in parliament but, with only 62.6 percent of the vote, it fell short of the two-thirds required to change the constitution.

On 10 May 1994, Nelson Mandela was inaugurated at a ceremony, outside the Union Buildings in Pretoria, attended by world leaders and watched on television by an estimated audience of one billion. Mandela rose magnificently to the occasion, delivering a speech that remains indelibly etched in the memories of all who heard it. In the following text, he invokes the land itself and acknowledges the divisions that almost tore it apart. He stresses that the future will be a time of reconciliation ('*the healing of the wounds*') between people of all races, and, in calling South Africa '*the rainbow nation*' uses the first of three phrases that have passed into common parlance. As he approaches the climactic moment, he begins four sentences with '*Let*' – a word with strong biblical overtones ('*Let there be light*'). Then, on the threshold of the final cadence point, he stalls to build tension, digressing momentarily to declare that no longer will his country be '*the skunk of the world*'. Finally, another '*Let*', the first of the three words for which he will above all be remembered.

Your Majesties, Your Highnesses, Distinguished Guests,
Comrades and Friends,

Today, all of us do, by our presence here, and by
our celebrations in other parts of our country
and the world, confer glory and hope to newborn
liberty. Out of the experience of an extraordinary
human disaster that lasted too long, must be born
a society of which all humanity will be proud.

Our daily deeds as ordinary South Africans must
produce an actual South African reality that will
reinforce humanity's belief in justice, strengthen its
confidence in the nobility of the human soul and
sustain all our hopes for a glorious life for all. All this
we owe both to ourselves and to the peoples of the
world who are so well represented here today.

To my compatriots, I have no hesitation in saying
that each one of us is as intimately attached to
the soil of this beautiful country as are the famous
jacaranda trees of Pretoria and the mimosa trees of
the bushveld. Each time one of us touches the soil
of this land, we feel a sense of personal renewal.
The national mood changes as the seasons change.

We are moved by a sense of joy and exhilaration
when the grass turns green and the flowers bloom.
That spiritual and physical oneness we all share with
this common homeland explains the depth of the
pain we all carried in our hearts as we saw our
country tear itself apart in a terrible conflict, and as
we saw it spurned, outlawed and isolated by the
peoples of the world, precisely because it has become
the universal base of the pernicious ideology and
practice of racism and racial oppression.

We, the people of South Africa, feel fulfilled that
humanity has taken us back into its bosom, that
we, who were outlaws not so long ago, have today
been given the rare privilege to be host to the
nations of the world on our own soil. We thank all
our distinguished international guests for having
come to take possession with the people of our
country of what is, after all, a common victory for
justice, for peace, for human dignity. We trust that
you will continue to stand by us as we tackle the
challenges of building peace, prosperity, non-sexism,
non-racialism and democracy.

We deeply appreciate the role that the masses of
our people and their political mass democratic,
religious, women, youth, business, traditional and

other leaders have played to bring about this conclusion. Not least among them is my Second Deputy President, the Honourable F.W. de Klerk. We would also like to pay tribute to our security forces, in all their ranks, for the distinguished role they have played in securing our first democratic elections and the transition to democracy, from blood-thirsty forces which still refuse to see the light. The time for the healing of the wounds has come. The moment to bridge the chasms that divide us has come. The time to build is upon us. We have, at last, achieved our political emancipation. We pledge ourselves to liberate all our people from the continuing bondage of poverty, deprivation, suffering, gender and other discrimination.

We succeeded to take our last steps to freedom in conditions of relative peace. We commit ourselves to the construction of a complete, just and lasting peace. We have triumphed in the effort to implant hope in the breasts of the millions of our people. We enter into a covenant that we shall build the society in which all South Africans, both black and white, will be able to walk tall, without any fear in their hearts, assured of their inalienable right to human dignity – a rainbow nation at peace with itself and the world.

As a token of its commitment to the renewal of our country, the new Interim Government of National Unity will, as a matter of urgency, address the issue of amnesty for various categories of our people who are currently serving terms of imprisonment.

We dedicate this day to all the heroes and heroines in this country and the rest of the world who sacrificed in many ways and surrendered their lives so that we could be free. Their dreams have become reality. Freedom is their reward. We are both humbled and elevated by the honour and privilege that you, the people of South Africa, have bestowed on us, as the first President of a united, democratic, non-racial and non-sexist government.

We understand it still that there is no easy road to freedom We know it well that none of us acting alone can achieve success. We must therefore act together as a united people, for national reconciliation, for nation building, for the birth of a new world.

Let there be justice for all.

Let there be peace for all.

Let there be work, bread, water and salt for all.

Let each know that for each the body, the mind and the soul have been freed to fulfill themselves.

Never, never and never again shall it be that this beautiful land will again experience the oppression of one by another and suffer the indignity of being the skunk of the world.

Let freedom reign.

The sun shall never set on so glorious a human achievement!

God bless Africa!
Thank you.

Chapter 4

President of South Africa (1994–99)

From any political perspective, Mandela's life as freedom fighter and long-term prisoner of apartheid had been a fairly straightforward narrative of good versus evil. As president of South Africa, Mandela entered a world of moral ambivalence in which good people might act reprehensibly and evil people might be redeemed through acts of exemplary virtuousness.

That Mandela was an acclaimed figurehead had been clear from the moment he walked out of Victor Verser (see page 76). Now aged 74, he could have restricted his role in office to attendance at ceremonial occasions and left the business of government to his two deputies, Thabo Mbeki and F.W. de Klerk. But he was determined to be an effective president. He was under no illusions about the challenge that faced him. He had to allay white fears of a black revolution and prevent a mass exodus of Europeans similar to that which had blighted Mozambique after independence from Portugal in 1975. He also had to make sure that the blacks did not think he was selling out. There were economic problems, too. When Mandela went to prison, South Africa prospered from high gold prices and cheap labour costs. By the time he came to power, the value of gold was low and domestic wages were higher than they had ever been.

Mandela adopted a conciliatory approach to the Afrikaners and the Europeans. He appointed National Party politicians to his cabinet. When warned by security advisers that an old Boer major on his personal staff had once bombed an ANC building, he airily dismissed their concerns, saying '*So what? I work in government with people who have done worse things than that*'. In his speeches – which were now written in consultation with a multi-racial team of advisers led by Joel Netshitenzhe (b. 1956; subsequently head of South Africa's Government Communication and Information Systems [GCIS]) – he stressed repeatedly that apartheid was a trauma for all South Africans, regardless of their colour.

Meanwhile, in speeches to predominantly black audiences, Mandela consistently rehearsed the miraculous story so far – the end of apartheid and the relatively peaceful transition to majority rule in less than five years. This constituency had growing concerns that its lot was not improving as quickly as had been hoped. Desmond Tutu (b. 1931; the first black Archbishop of Cape Town) publicly voiced the suspicion that the new government had '*stopped the gravy train long enough to get on it*'. But Mandela himself remained immune to such criticism – partly because of his personal history and partly because of his austere lifestyle, which was largely unaltered by his rise from prisoner to president.

Although the overall tenor of Mandela's public pronouncements while in office was positive and exhortatory, he never hesitated to tackle the negative aspects of life in democratic South Africa.

Strengthening Ties
ANC Conference, Bloemfontein,
17 December 1994

After seven months in power, Mandela opened the 49th ANC annual conference. His long, detailed speech – the antithesis of sloganeering and soundbite politics – to a predominantly black audience begins with a reminder of the distance travelled and expresses gratitude to foreign supporters of his Government of National Unity (GNU). The main theme, however, is the problems caused by the appointment of National Party members to the new government and the maintenance of old-guard Afrikaner bureaucrats in the posts they held under apartheid. Was this, he asks, a terrible misjudgement? After a typically history-based opening, Mandela acknowledges that mistakes were made but persuasively justifies the overall policy.

For the first time in the history of our country, we have under one roof, sharing the same vision and planning as equals, delegates from every sector of South African society, including those who hold the highest offices in the land. This in itself vividly captures the qualitative change our country has undergone: a dream fulfilled and a pledge redeemed.

That pledge, made in this mother-city of the ANC 83 years ago... was to transform South Africa into a non-racial and democratic society. As we meet in the environs where they planted the seed, we can proudly say to the founders: the country is in the hands of the people; the tree of liberty is firmly rooted in the soil of the motherland!

This Conference is the first such assembly after our momentous elections, the convention which signals the closing of a painful and yet glorious chapter in the history of our country and our organization, and the opening of a new chapter of freedom, dignity and prosperity...

... While we can confidently say that the transformation that has taken place vindicates this conclusion, we should also admit that, in the process, we did also falter. What is crucial though is whether we were able to learn from our mistakes and to adapt our approach to a changing and dynamic situation... We should take this opportunity to thank the international community for the magnificent role they played in helping steer our transition... We chose deliberately to resume negotiations with the NP [National Party] government first, before multi-party discussions...

Our decision to proceed in this manner was premised on the understanding that the ANC and

the NP government were the major players in the
transition. This was because, on the one hand, the
ANC was the premier liberation movement; and on
the other, the NP was the administration in power.
The two parties differed fundamentally on the basic
questions facing the country. Yet, they had to cooperate
to ensure implementation of decisions the NP
government was forced to agree to in negotiations.

The situation had to be handled in such a manner
that we could tactfully persuade the leading forces
within the NP that the transition was also in their
interests; to assist them in appreciating the need to
close a treacherous chapter in South Africa's history.
Transition with the minimum of disruption required
their cooperation. This did not mean a submerging
of the fundamental contradictions; but it helped pave
the way for the final settlement...

However, lurking in the background were the
extreme right-wingers whose politics of desperation
centred around crude maintenance of the status quo,
racism, tribal chauvinism and violence. Their alliance,
though representing a small fraction of society, was
made the more dangerous because it included
elements in the state apparatus, bantustan power
bases and, with some of them, potent issues to
mobilize backward forces within society.

Our approach to engage these forces helped weaken
their cohesion and resolve. Insofar as the white
right is concerned, we persisted with discussions
which culminated in compromises offering them
a feeling of security and a constitutional channel to
address their apprehensions. The more far-sighted

among them do realize that it was not all in vain, and they are cooperating with us in search of a stable and prosperous future for all our people...

In engaging these forces, we had also noted that prominent forces within the regime's security establishment either hid behind the extreme right wing or themselves engineered some of the disruptive actions. We can today reveal that, especially in the build-up to election day, we had to engage some of these elements and secure a commitment that they would act in defence of the process. We did so to save lives and secure our people's right to a democratic election...

At the same time, serious weaknesses in a number of areas were exposed. One of them, whose significance transcends narrow interests of the ANC, is the extent to which particularly poorer sections of the Coloured and Indian communities found solace in the racist mobilization of the National Party, and voted in a manner that demonstrated fear of their counterparts among Africans. For a start, this demonstrated weaknesses in our message and organization. It also brought out in sharp relief a reality that we barely wished to admit. In class terms, it is a tragedy that working people from these communities should respond with fear to the prospect of their brothers and sisters attaining equality.

Like a predator at the smell of blood, the National Party latched onto this, and it continues to do so today, an exercise which can only widen the racial chasm. It is also a challenge to us that, while many whites recognized the legitimacy of the ANC and correctness of its positions, they chose to vote on the basis of racial sentiment.

This therefore makes the challenge of deracializing South African society one of the most important campaigns we have to undertake. Our nation shall never truly come of its own if the racial compartments apartheid has imposed on us, both in our way of thinking and physical areas of abode, are not eradicated...

These are some of the challenges that we will need to keep in mind.... It is quite clear, without preempting discussion in the relevant commissions, that we should not allow any political provocation to distract us from our central message that, together, we should build a better life for all...

In this respect, we need to avoid two extremes. The one is to conclude that we are merely in political office – weak, tied hand and foot by some terrible agreements that we reached in negotiations. This then leads to a tendency to pander to the resistance to change by the NP, IFP [Inkatha Freedom Party], DP [Democratic Party] and other parties and elements in the state machinery.

The other extreme is to create the impression that we are all-powerful, ready to realize each and every one of the programmes we would like to implement. This then leads to populist and ambitious pronouncements that have nothing to do with objective reality, only to retreat in embarrassment down the line... South Africa has undergone its most fundamental political transformation in centuries. But the socio-economic problems arising from colonial domination remain as stark as they were under apartheid. To refer to the five million unemployed, the seven million without real housing and the millions who are illiterate, is to state the obvious yet daunting challenges.

Truth and Reconciliation

Cape Town, 9 February 1996

At the official opening of the third session of parliament, Mandela made a long and wide-ranging speech about South Africa's achievements since the election and the challenges that faced it in the future. He also spoke about the Truth and Reconciliation Commission (TRC), which had been set up in the previous year under Archbishop Tutu. The purpose of the TRC – to investigate atrocities during the apartheid era – had always been clear but its terms of reference had been one of the major sticking points in the discussions leading up to the ANC takeover from the National Party. F.W. de Klerk called for a general amnesty; the most radical members of the ANC and Inkatha wanted vengeance. But Mandela steadfastly maintained that the former was impossible as well as distasteful, and that the latter would create martyrs and perpetuate the abuses that he was committed to end. In the event, the TRC had the power to grant amnesty to those found to have committed '*gross violations of human rights*' under extenuating circumstances.

By the time the TRC concluded its investigations in 1999, it had granted around 150 such pardons to more than 7,000 applicants. The Commission was subjected to constant criticism by the National Party, which denounced it as a tool of the ANC, and by radical blacks, many of whom thought that it was a murderers' charter and some of whom refused to seek amnesty on the grounds that theirs had been a just struggle. Nevertheless, the commission is widely regarded as the outstanding achievement of Mandela's presidency.

Mandela starts on a strongly positive note, paying tribute to his nation's sporting achievements – recent triumphs in football and rugby were made even sweeter because South Africa, for so long '*the skunk of the world*' (as referred to in Mandela's inaugural speech; see pages 88–93), had been the host of two international tournaments. What follows is classic Mandela: form is subordinated to substance as the body of the speech contains a wealth of detail about various new measures and initiatives; there are few rhetorical flourishes other than the repetitions of the key concept of '*healing and building*' and the three passages that begin with '*We can neither…*'.

Today in the streets of Johannesburg, the New Patriotism of our new democracy once again asserts itself as citizens of that city express their appreciation for the feat of our soccer team in the African Nations Cup [on 3 February, the hosts had beaten Tunisia 2–0 in the final of the competition]. This is bound to replay itself in other cities, adding to the crowning glory of our rugby world champions [host nation South Africa had beaten New Zealand 15–12 in the final on 24 June 1995].

Our sportspersons are performing beyond the nation's wildest expectations. On and off the field, they are uniting our nation like never before, by their determination to do the best for their country.

Such is the true character of South Africans. We do possess the inner strength to achieve excellence. We have the will to persevere against all odds.

We enter 1996… faced with the challenge of bringing these positive qualities to bear on every thing we do: to make South Africa a winning nation.
We must bring out the best in all of us; and, like our sportspersons, perform better everywhere:

- to expand the economy and create jobs;
- to improve the quality of life for all;
- to expand the frontiers of freedom; and
- to ensure comprehensive security for all citizens.

These are the critical challenges that we face within and outside these hallowed chambers.

In October this year, we shall pass the halfway mark of the present legislature and its executive. The nation and the world will judge us not on whether we mean to do good; but, above all, on whether we have mobilized South Africans to work together to improve their quality of life…

At last, millions who had no hope in the future can look ahead with confidence in the full knowledge that they have a government prepared to work together with them to build a better life for all.

We formally start the third session of the democratic parliament with South Africa's economy healthier than in many decades...We enter 1996 with no hesitation about the extent to which democracy has taken root in our society...

Yes, South Africa is not only on the right road. We are well on our way to making this the country of our dreams. I take the opportunity to congratulate all South Africans, in the public and private sectors – the most prominent in the land as well as the humble member of the community – all of whom are striving to add another brick to the edifice of our democracy. We have set out on this road together, and we should together aim for the stars...

If these achievements are something to be proud of, this is because they have laid the foundation to make a real impact on the iniquities of the past. For we are only at the beginning of a long journey... that requires thorough planning and tenacious industry, if we are to remain on course and capable of sustaining our march.

Let me preface the identification of the challenges of the coming year by saying that all of us, all South Africans, are called upon to become builders and healers. But, for all the joy and excitement of creation, to build and to heal are difficult undertakings. We can neither heal nor build, if such healing and building are perceived as one-way...

with the victims of past injustices forgiving and the beneficiaries merely content in gratitude. Together we must set out to correct the defects of the past.

We can neither heal nor build, if on the one hand, the rich in our society see the poor as hordes of irritants; or if, on the other hand, the poor sit back, expecting charity. All of us must take responsibility for the upliftment of our conditions, prepared to give our best to the benefit of all.

We can neither heal nor build if we continue to have people in positions of influence and power who, at best, pay lip service to affirmative action, black empowerment and the emancipation of women, or who are, in reality, opposed to these goals; if we have people who continue with blind arrogance to practice racism in the work-places and schools, despite the appeal we made in our very first address to this parliament. We must work together to ensure the equitable distribution of wealth, opportunity and power in our society.

We cannot build or heal our nation if... we continue with business as usual, wallowing in notions of the past. Everywhere and in everything we do, what is now required is boldness in thinking, firmness in resolve and consistency in action.... But let us be brutally frank.

Despite the welcome rate of growth, very few jobs have been created. In fact, against the backdrop of new entrants into the job market, there has been a shrinkage in opportunities. We need a national vision to lift us out of this quagmire.

If we do not act together in the public and private sectors to develop and implement such a national strategic vision, the danger is that even the modest growth we have attained, will peter out in a matter of a few years, as the strain of limited capacity, skills shortage, balance of payments and other constraints start to gather momentum; and as increasing unemployment and accelerating poverty bear down on our society.

To move forward with purpose requires that we extricate the public and private sectors from the current comfort zones, and break through the threshold to achieve a rate of growth sufficient to create jobs, and generate resources for rapid socio-economic programmes to uplift the poor...

It is the firm view of the Government of National Unity that the growth and development strategy should be pursued in an integrated manner. We do not subscribe to the notion that growth on its own can rectify the backlogs of apartheid in a mysterious trickle-down fashion. In any case, in our skewed social structure, there cannot be growth without development...

The question needs to be posed, whether we do... have a state machinery capable of meeting the objectives of growth and development... Let us remind ourselves of this government's mandate, which is to establish a single, streamlined, efficient and transparent Public Service and to allocate more public resources to capital expenditure. Let us be frank and say that the current service is too large... it has to be rationalized. There is no other option.

However, our actions cannot ignore the painful truth that the most affected will be areas that are poor, with low economic activity and little prospect for alternative employment. This means, among other things, searching for creative negotiated solutions that will help stimulate economic activity.

The rationalization process will not be vindictive. Neither will it be carried out in a haphazard manner. Rather, it will affect all races and provinces… The national effort to improve the quality of life of the people means also that each citizen and each community should enjoy security in the home, at work and in the streets…

If, during the course of the past year, South Africa afforded its citizens unprecedented freedom and a human rights culture, the frontiers are bound to widen immeasurably in 1996. The New Patriotism, abroad in our nation, is a reflection of how liberating democracy is, for all our citizens in their rainbow colours.

No longer is the state a mighty colossus intimidating everyone in its wake. The openness in this and other legislatures, the transparency of the executive and the participatory style of government – all these have given practical meaning to the concept of government by the people, for the people…

The Truth and Reconciliation Commission will help cement democracy by laying bare that which our nation should never again experience. It will entrench justice by affording victims the

reparations due to them. It will, through this, and by means of amnesty, ensure lasting reconciliation.

As with other such institutions, the Truth and Reconciliation Commission will succeed only if it gets the cooperation of all of us. I call on all South Africans to respect the Commission's independence and impartiality, its integrity and good faith. The Commissioners themselves have reiterated what the founding legislation pronounces, that the aim of their work is justice and reconciliation, not vengeance…

Farewell Speech to Parliament
Cape Town, 26 March 1999

On 9 May 1997, F.W. de Klerk's National Party withdrew from the Government of National Unity. On 18 July 1998, his 80th birthday, Nelson Mandela was married for the third time, to Graça, the widow of Samora Machel (1933–86), the former president of Mozambique and an ANC ally who had been killed in a mysterious air crash in South Africa. In August, Mandela announced his decision to step down as ANC president and not to seek re-election as state president at the end of his five-year term in 1999.

Seven months later, at the final sitting of the first democratically elected government of South Africa, Mandela brought the curtain down on his political career with a speech that was a tour

de force, with historical references, hope for the future, geniality and a greater than usual number of conventional rhetorical devices, notably the four invitations to his audience to '*Look*' and the stylized uses of the verb 'to count' as he enumerates his blessings: two instances of '*I count myself*' followed by '*I will count myself*' and '*I will then count myself*'.

… This day is a moment of deep significance for all of us whom the people of South Africa have entrusted with representing their needs and interests, their aspirations and hopes… In brief, we have laid the foundation for a better life. Things that were unimaginable a few years ago have become everyday reality. And of this we must be proud.

Questions have been raised, we know, as to whether this House is not a carriage on the gravy train [see page 99], whose passengers idle away their time at the nation's expense.

To those who raise such questions we say: Look at the record of our Parliament during these first years of freedom.

Look at the work of the nation's representatives when they formed themselves into a Constitutional Assembly. With a breadth of consultation and public participation that few would have imagined possible, and in a spirit of unprecedented consensus-seeking, it was here that a constitution was formulated and adopted to enshrine our people's deepest aspirations. Look at the one hundred laws on average that have been passed by this legislature each year.

These have been no trivial laws nor mere adjustments to an existing body of statutes. They have created a framework for the revolutionary transformation of society and of government itself, so that the legacy of our past can be undone and put right. It was here that the possibility was created of improving the lives and working conditions of millions.

Look at the work of the committees that have scrutinized legislation and improved it, posed difficult questions of the executive and given the public insight and oversight of government as never before. This is a record in which we can take pride... Each historical period defines specific challenges of national progress and leadership; and no man is an island.

As for me personally, I belong to the generation of leaders for whom the achievement of democracy was the defining challenge. I count myself fortunate in not having had to experience the rigours of exile and decades of underground and mass struggles that consumed the lives of such giants as Oliver Tambo...

I count myself fortunate that, amongst that generation, history permitted me to take part in South Africa's transition from that period into the new era whose foundation we have been laying together.

I hope that decades from now, when history is written, the role of that generation will be appreciated, and that I will not be found wanting against the measure of their fortitude and vision...

To the extent that I have been able to achieve
anything, I know that this is because I am the
product of the people of South Africa. I am the
product of the rural masses who inspired in me the
pride in our past and the spirit of resistance. I am the
product of the workers of South Africa who, in the
mines, factories, fields and offices of our country,
have pursued the principle that the interests of each
are founded in the common interest of all. I am the
product of South Africa's intelligentsia, of every
colour, who have laboured to give our society
knowledge of itself and to fashion our people's
aspirations into a realizable dream. I am the product
of South Africa's business people – in industry and
agriculture, commerce and finance – whose spirit of
enterprise has helped turn our country's immense
natural resources into the wealth of our nation.

To the extent that I have been able to take
our country forward to this new era it is
because I am the product of the people of the
world who have cherished the vision of a better
life for all people everywhere. They insisted, in
a spirit of self-sacrifice, that that vision should
be realized in South Africa too. They gave us
hope because we knew by their solidarity that
our ideas could not be silenced since they were
the ideas of all humanity.

I am the product of Africa and her long-cherished
dream of a rebirth that can now be realized so that
all of her children may play in the sun.

If I have been able to help take our country a
few steps towards democracy, non-racialism and

non-sexism, it is because I am a product of the African National Congress, of the movement for justice, dignity and freedom that produced countless giants in whose shadow we find our glory...

When, as will be the case in a few months, I once again become an ordinary citizen of our land, it shall be as one whose concerns and capacities are shaped by the people of our land.

I will count myself as amongst the aged of our society; as one of the rural population; as one concerned for the children and youth of our country; and as a citizen of the world committed, as long as I have strength, to work for a better life for all people everywhere. And as I have always done, I will do what I can within the discipline of the broad movement for peace and democracy to which I belong.

I will then count myself amongst the ordinary men and women whose well being must, in any country, be the standard by which democratic government must be judged...

It is a measure of our success as a nation that an international community that inspired hope in us, in turn itself finds hope in how we overcame the divisions of centuries by reaching out to one another. To the extent that we have been able to reciprocate in renewing hope amongst the people of the world, we are grateful indeed and feel doubly blessed. And it goes without saying that we should all live up to those expectations which the world has of us...

To the extent that we have still to reconcile and heal our nation; to the extent that the consequences of apartheid still permeate our society and define the lives of millions of South Africans as lives of deprivation, those challenges are unchanged...

Amongst the principles which the liberation movement pursued from the beginning of negotiations is that out of any debate we must emerge stronger and more united, and that there should be no winners or losers.

Deputy President Thabo Mbeki, whom we all expect to be the President of South Africa, exemplifies this approach which is critical to the unity of our country. I call on all to give their support to his leadership, across all political parties. His and other voices are those of a new generation of leaders that are emerging in answer to new historical challenges. They are the voices of the good men and women who exist in all communities and all parties, and who define themselves as leaders by their capacity to identify the issues that unite us as a nation.

Together, we must continue our efforts to turn our hopes into reality.

The long walk continues.

Chapter 5

In Retirement
(1999–)

After deciding not to seek a second term in office, Nelson Mandela withdrew from active politics in June 1999. He was succeeded as president of South Africa by Thabo Mbeki, the winner of that year's election.

Mandela returned to live in Qunu, the rural village in the Eastern Cape where he had spent the happiest days of his childhood, but he did not disappear from sight. He travelled widely, partly because he was still in enormous demand with everyone from insecure politicians who wanted to bask in his reflected glory to ordinary young people who idolized him. The other main reason for his continued globetrotting was that, quite simply, he enjoyed it. Mandela the showman loved the adoration and, even in his eighties, Mandela the innocent just liked seeing the world.

In 2000, Mandela acted as a mediator in war-torn Burundi. He maintained an active role in the Nelson Mandela Children's Fund, which he had set up on becoming president in 1994 and into which he had paid one third of his salary throughout his term of office. He also raised funds for the Nelson Mandela Foundation to promote social justice, and in 2002 founded a global HIV/AIDS charity, named 46664, his old prison number.

What mainly characterizes Mandela's speeches in retirement is the evident reduction in the pressure on him to be both a statesman and a politician. Now he is at liberty to present the broad historical sweep that had long been his forté without the need to acknowledge every shade of opinion. When he feels moved to express his own views, he does so trenchantly, particularly regarding the Iraq War (p. 131).

Support for Successor

13th International AIDS Conference,
Durban, 14 July 2000

Mandela may have retired from the political arena but here he returned to it to support Thabo Mbeki, who had caused controversy in April 2000 by questioning whether HIV caused AIDS. Already heavily involved in work for related charities, Mandela took this closing speech as an opportunity to express his view that the crisis was too grave for reflection on its causes and that all available resources should be channelled into minimizing its effects. Note in the second paragraph how Mandela switches unaccountably from the first person singular to the first person plural. He had grappled before with the mutable significance of 'I' and 'we' in different contexts, and had used the latter in any that related to the ANC,

development resources have to be diverted to
deal with the consequences of the pandemic…

Earlier this week we were shocked to learn that
within South Africa one in two, that is half, of our
young people will die of AIDS. The most frightening
thing is that all of these infections which statistics tell
us about, and the attendant human suffering, could
have been, can be, prevented…

Earlier this week we were shocked to learn that
within South Africa one in two, that is half, of our
young people will die of AIDS. The most frightening
thing is that all of these infections which statistics tell
us about, and the attendant human suffering, could
have been, can be, prevented…

The experience in a number of countries has
taught that HIV infection can be prevented
through investing in information and life skills
development for young people… Stigma and
discrimination can be stopped; new infections can
be prevented; and the capacity of families and
communities to care for people living with HIV
and AIDS can be enhanced.

It is not, I must add, as if the South African
government has not moved significantly on many
of these areas… The challenge is to move from
rhetoric to action. and action at an unprecedented

We need bold initiatives to prevent new infections among young people, and large-scale actions to prevent mother-to-child transmission, and at the same time we need to continue the international effort of searching for appropriate vaccines;

We need to aggressively treat opportunistic infections; and We need to work with families and communities to care for children and young people to protect them from violence and abuse, and to ensure that they grow up in a safe and supportive environment. For this there is need for us to be focussed, to be strategic, and to mobilize all of our resources and alliances, and to sustain the effort until this war is won.

...Others will not save us if we do not primarily commit ourselves. Let us, however, not underestimate the resources required to conduct this battle. Partnership with the international community is vital. A constant theme in all our messages has been that in this interdependent and globalized world, we have indeed again become the keepers of our brother and sister. That cannot be more graphically the case than in the common fight against HIV/AIDS...

Funeral Tribute to Walter Sisulu

Croesus Cemetery, Bo̶̶̶̶̶̶̶̶̶̶̶̶ burg, weeks later, Mandela made a short oration in memory of his friend and mentor. Powered by a sense of loss and by the speaker's own feelings of mortality, the speech is strengthened by minimal rhetorical embellishment. Among the few flourishes are the reference to '*a long road*' – an allusion both to life as a whole and to the title of Mandela's autobiography – and the figurative use of the word '*spears*' as a metonym for the old guard of *Umkhonto we Sizwe*.

In the last few years we have walked this road with greater frequency, marching in the procession to bid farewell to the veterans of our movement, paying our last respects to the fallen spears of the nation from a generation now reaching the end of a long and heroic struggle.

Those of us from that generation, who are singled out to stay the longest, have to bear the pain of seeing our comrades go. We shared tears over them because we have walked such a long road together: sharing trials and tribulations; danger, anguish and fear; and also precious moments of joy, gladness and laughter. Their going must leave an emptiness with those of us who stay be hind.

Our sadness over them is tempered by the comforting knowledge that the separation will now not be interminably long. And more importantly, by the sure knowledge that their lives were not wasted and spent fruitlessly. They fought a noble battle and lived their lives in pursuit of a better life for all who follow. The democracy in which we bury them and honour

them, is the sweet fruit of their lives of struggle
and sacrifice.

Today we stand at the grave of one of the greatest
amongst that generation of great freedom fighters.
We take leave of a man of whom I have already
said in these sad days since his death, that from
the moment when we first met he has been my
friend, my brother, my keeper, my comrade... A
part of us is gone with his passing...

His greatness as a leader derived from his humility
and his ingrained belief in and respect for collective
leadership. He knew and taught us that wisdom
comes from sharing insights and listening to and
learning from each other. He was always the unifier,
never a divider...

The spear of the nation has fallen, as the militant
youth of our country once sang during funerals. Let
us pick up the spear, now to build a country after
the example that Walter Sisulu has set for us...

Democratic Decade

Cape Town, 10 May 2004

Exactly 10 years after Nelson Mandela was
inaugurated, he returned to Parliament to
deliver a commemorative address in which he
reviewed the past and surveyed the future. He also
used his status as a world statesman to comment
on the 2003 invasion of Iraq by the United States

**and Britain. In retirement, he has no need to wrap
his thoughts in diplomatic language – he
disapproves of the military adventure and says so in
unequivocal terms.**

... On this exact day 10 years ago democratic
South Africa celebrated its ceremonial birth with
the inauguration of its first President and two
Deputy Presidents [Thabo Mbeki and F.W. de
Klerk]. We recall the joy and excitement of a
nation that had found itself: the collective relief
that we had stepped out of our restrictive past and
the expectant air of walking into a brighter future.
The national climate was one of magnanimity
and a great generosity of spirit. As a people we
were enormously proud of what we had achieved,
negotiating amongst ourselves a peaceful resolution
to what was regarded as one of the most intractable
situations of conflict in the world.

We were not unaware of or blind to the extent,
depth and gravity of the challenges ahead of us as
we set out on that day to transform, reconstruct
and develop our nation and our society. However,
the overwhelming feelings in those early days
of democratic nationhood were of hope and
confidence. We had miraculously... transcended the
deep divisions of our past to create a new inclusive
democratic order; we had confidence that as a
nation we would similarly confront and deal with
the challenges of reconstruction and development...

Merely observing this parliament inspires national
pride and confidence. We, the people of South
Africa, the Preamble to our Constitution states,

believe that South Africa belongs to all who live in it, united in our diversity. The make-up of this Parliament confirms that the people of South Africa had spoken in all its diversity, asserting the strength of our unity in diversity...

... [W]hat do I wish for our democracy in this second decade that we have entered? Let us never be unmindful of the terrible past from which we come – that memory not as a means to keep us shackled to the past in a negative manner, but rather as a joyous reminder of how far we have come and how much we have achieved. The memory of a history of division and hate, injustice and suffering, inhumanity of person against person should inspire us to celebrate our own demonstration of the capacity of human beings to progress, to go forward, to improve, to do better...

... A guiding principle in our search for and establishment of a non-racial inclusive democracy in our country has been that there are good men and women to be found in all groups and from all sectors of society; and that in an open and free society those South Africans will come together to jointly and cooperatively realize the common good.

My wish is that South Africans never give up on the belief in goodness, that they cherish that faith in human beings as a cornerstone of our democracy. The first value mentioned under the founding principles of our Constitution is that of human dignity. We accord persons dignity by assuming that they are good, that they share the human qualities we ascribe to ourselves. Historical enemies [the National Party and the ANC-led opposition] succeeded in negotiating a peaceful transition from apartheid to democracy exactly because we were prepared to accept the inherent capacity for goodness in the other.

We live in a world where there is enough reason for cynicism and despair. We watch as two of the leading democracies, two leading nations of the free world, get involved in a war that the United Nations did not sanction; we look on with horror as reports surface of terrible abuses against the dignity of human beings held captive by invading forces in their own country. We see how the powerful countries – all of them democracies – manipulate multilateral bodies to the great disadvantage and suffering of the poorer developing nations. There is enough reason for cynicism and despair. But then we should take heart from our own experience and performance…

In a cynical world we have become an inspiration to many. We signal that good can be achieved amongst human beings who are prepared to trust, prepared to believe in the goodness of people…

Make Poverty History
Trafalgar Square, London, 3 February 2005

Having been diagnosed, in 2003, with prostate cancer, Mandela attended events only when compelled by conscience. One such occasion was a rally for Make Poverty History (a coalition of British- and Irish-based relief charities; part of the Global Campaign for Action Against Poverty), which was held on the eve of a meeting in London of the G7 (the finance ministers of the world's main industrial nations, Britain, Canada, France, Germany, Italy, Japan and the United States). Mandela flew to England and made a rousing short speech about the plight of the world's poor and the moral obligation of the haves to care for the have-nots. His use of the word *'chains'* is both literal and an allusion to the famous remark of Jean-Jacques Rousseau (1712–78; Swiss-born French philosopher) at the beginning of *The Social Contract*: *'Man was born free, and everywhere he is in chains'*.

... As you know, I recently formally announced my retirement from public life and should really not be here. However, as long as poverty, injustice and gross inequality persist in our world, none of us can truly rest...

Massive poverty and obscene inequality are such terrible scourges of our times – times in which the world boasts breathtaking advances in science, technology, industry and wealth accumulation – that they have to rank alongside slavery and apartheid as social evils.

The Global Campaign for Action Against Poverty can take its place as a public movement alongside the movement to abolish slavery and the international solidarity against apartheid.

And I can never thank the people of Britain enough for their support through those days of the struggle against apartheid. Many stood in solidarity with us, just a few yards from this spot.

Through your will and passion, you assisted in consigning that evil system forever to history. But in this new century, millions of people in the world's poorest countries remain imprisoned, enslaved, and in chains. They are trapped in the prison of poverty. It is time to set them free.

Like slavery and apartheid, poverty is not natural. It is man-made and it can be overcome and eradicated by the actions of human beings.

And overcoming poverty is not a gesture of charity. It is an act of justice. It is the protection of a fundamental human right, the right to dignity and a decent life. While poverty persists, there is no true freedom.

The steps that are needed from the developed nations are clear.

The first is ensuring trade justice. I have said before that trade justice is a truly meaningful way for the developed countries to show commitment to bringing about an end to global poverty.

The second is an end to the debt crisis for the poorest countries.

The third is to deliver much more aid and make sure it is of the highest quality.

In 2005, there is a unique opportunity for making an impact...

Tomorrow, here in London, the G7 finance ministers can make a significant beginning. I am happy to have been invited to meet with them... I say to all those leaders: do not look the other way; do not hesitate. Recognize that the world is hungry for action, not words. Act with courage and vision...

Sometimes it falls upon a generation to be great. You can be that great generation. Let your greatness blossom.

Of course the task will not be easy. But not to do this would be a crime against humanity, against which I ask all humanity now to rise up.

Make Poverty History in 2005. Make History in 2005. Then we can all stand with our heads held high.

Grateful Valediction

Hyde Park, London, 28 June 2008

As he approached his 90th birthday, Nelson Mandela returned to London to attend an open-air concert in Hyde Park in his honour. A crowd of 50,000 watched performances by a range of pop stars including Annie Lennox, Leona Lewis, Amy Winehouse and Dame Shirley Bassey,

before the former president came on stage to a
rapturous ovation.

In the following extract he refers gratefully to the
Free Nelson Mandela concert held at Wembley
Stadium, London, in 1988. Then, acknowledging
his own great age, Mandela passes on
responsibility for raising awareness of injustice,
poverty and disease to younger generations. Even
here, he makes reference to the importance of
freedom and democracy for all.

… Many years ago there was a historic concert
which called for our freedom. Your voices carried
across the water and inspired us in our prison cells
far away.

Tonight we can stand before you, free…

But even as we celebrate, let us remind ourselves
that our work is far from complete.

Where there is poverty and sickness, including
AIDS, where human beings are being oppressed,
there is more work to be done. Our work is for
freedom for all…

We say tonight after nearly 90 years of life, it is
time for new hands to lift the burdens.

It is in your hands now, I thank you.

Acknowledgements

The author and the publishers would like to extend their grateful thanks to the Nelson Mandela Foundation for their generous help in compiling this book. All speeches, with the exception of those listed below, are taken from that site.

p. 28, 29: From *Long Walk to Freedom* by Nelson Mandela. Copyright © 1994, 1995 by Nelson Rolihlahla Mandela. By permission of Little, Brown & Company.

Photographic credits
Front cover © Hans Gedda/Sygma/Corbis
p.6 Getty Images
p.14 Getty Images
p.26 Getty Images
p.30 Gideon Mendel/CORBIS
p.74 Time & Life Pictures/Getty Images
p.98 Gideon Mendel/CORBIS
p.113 AFP/Getty Images
p.120 Getty Images